MAKING A COMPLETE WARDROBE FROM 4 BASIC PATTERNS

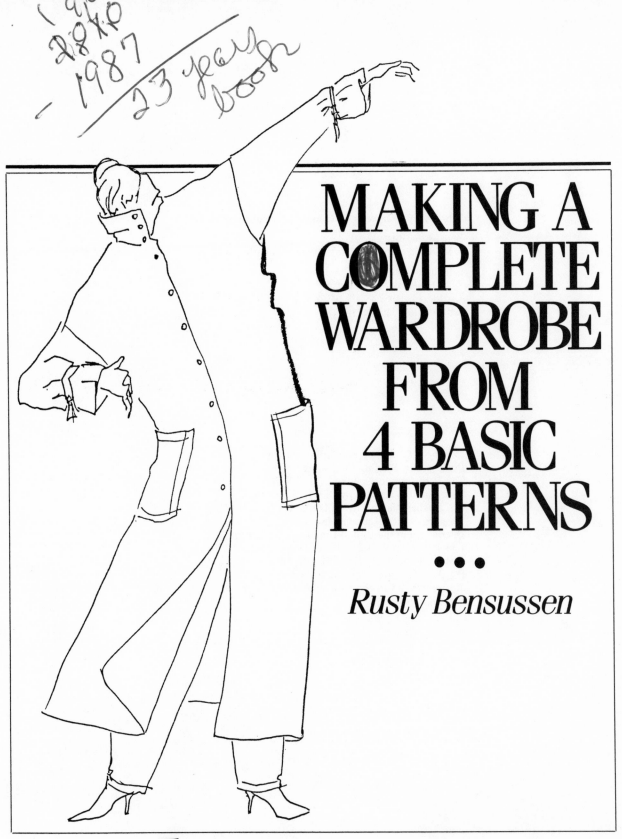

MAKING A COMPLETE WARDROBE FROM 4 BASIC PATTERNS

•••

Rusty Bensussen

Sterling Publishing Co., Inc. New York

Library of Congress Cataloging-in-Publication Data

Bensussen, Rusty.
  Making a complete wardrobe from 4 basic patterns.

  Includes index.
  1. Dressmaking.   I. Title.
TT515.B44   1987   646.4'304   86-23145
ISBN 0-8069-6464-2 (pbk.)

Copyright © 1987 by Estelle Bensussen
Published by Sterling Publishing Co., Inc.
Two Park Avenue, New York, N.Y. 10016
Distributed in Canada by Oak Tree Press Ltd.
℅ Canadian Manda Group, P.O. Box 920, Station U
Toronto, Ontario, Canada M8Z 5P9
Distributed in the United Kingdom by Blandford Press
Link House, West Street, Poole, Dorset BH15 1LL, England
Distributed in Australia by Capricorn Ltd.
P.O. Box 665, Lane Cove, NSW 2066
Manufactured in the United States of America

Contents

ACKNOWLEDGMENTS

A special *thank you* to the following people who have so generously contributed their eyes, ears and expertise to this book:

Gayle Carrol and Wendy Bensussen-Walls, my daughters, mentors and critics; Ed Bensussen, my husband, who is still hoping that I'll find time to make dinner instead of reservations; and Caryl Weldon, professional color consultant and especially helpful friend. I might have done it without you . . . but unquestionably, not nearly as well.

Sincerely,
E.B.

Fig. 1.   Playing "dress-up."

Introduction

Dress-up is a game we play as children (Fig. 1). We borrow freely from the adult finery of bygone eras, lovingly stowed in trunk and storage bag, attic, and closet, creating wardrobes with imagination and élan. But what happens to us as we grow up? Following the uniform of the day, we crawl into a shell of conservatism and the fear of being different from the crowd. We copy the wardrobes of friends or neighbors, trading imagination, fun, and personal identity for conformity and boredom. Falling into the trap of sameness, we dress like everyone else (Fig. 2).

When we receive an invitation to a party, why do we often call friends with that stock question, "What are you going to wear?" What difference does it really make? Our friends probably don't find comfort in the same clothes we enjoy, anyhow.

Clothes can be fun; if you let them. They can make a personal statement, brighten your day with wonderful colors, and create a mood, an aura of individual style. A trip to your closet can be like a trip to a deli where you can find variety, spice, and color, and can experience a sense of adventure. An exhilarating sensation comes over you when you're making your own choices.

When you first started to sew, you undoubtedly said, "Now I can make all the beautiful clothes I've always wanted." What happened to all those plans and dreams? For openers, you probably went

Fig. 2. Conformity dressing.

9

shopping for patterns with a strong-willed, well-meaning friend who promptly imposed her choices on you. You then compromised your fabric choices—after a consensus—and gave up your personal color choices in favor of popular opinion.

Now the time has come to put the fun back into your life; to sew with imagination from personal choices; to start dressing to please yourself; to re-examine that dream wardrobe you carefully laid to rest because you were afraid to look different.

A dream wardrobe doesn't have to stay hidden under your pillow, nor should your plans for it fade with the light of day. It can flow from a few simple patterns, fill your closet with wearable choices, and span the seasons. A dream wardrobe can enhance your life by giving you the clothing versatility and uniqueness you've always desired.

Your dream wardrobe can come together in cotton, linen, wool, silk, leather, or synthetics, or any combination of the above (Fig. 3). It can include fashionable separates or one-piece costumes, but it must be *your* wardrobe, *your* choice. Best of all, your wardrobe can be created from these four easy-fitting patterns: a *top, two skirts,* and *a pair of pants* (Fig. 4).

Fig. 3. Dream wardrobe.

Each pattern will not only yield the original design, it can be used to create many additional garments. A pattern can be versatile: It can lend itself to new directions; be the basis of more than one look; serve for multiple designs without any physical changes. Each of the patterns in this book fills these requirements. They are the basic patterns that you will create from the enclosed charts. The list of garments that can result is almost endless.

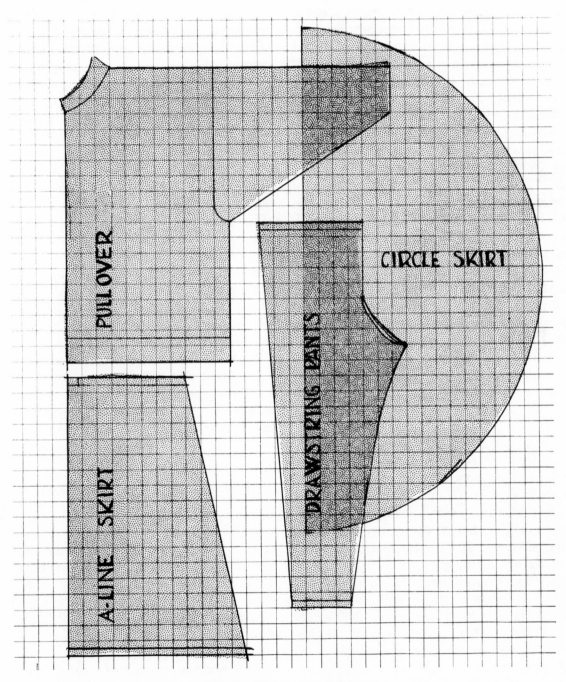

Fig. 4.   The four patterns.

We'll start with the pullover. This pattern, as with each pattern in this book, will be fully explored for the maximum number of variations and the maximum use. Extended styles include a tunic, dress, caftan, evening gown, jacket, vest, coat, and more.

Of the two skirt patterns from which to choose, a softly fitting A-line and a full, sweeping circle skirt, either could be the mainstay of your wardrobe. Each of these styles can be worn to the office, a meeting, dinner, the theatre, or the market. The A-line can be slimmed for a straighter look or widened for a softer flow of fabric. It can be shortened to a miniskirt or lengthened to barely brush the floor. Either skirt pattern can be combined with the pullover pattern to become a dress—a spinoff for a whole new series of designs.

The circle skirt lends itself to cottons, woollens, and sheers. It can be made in a practical street length or cut longer to swirl gracefully around your ankles. Any length you choose for this style will be feminine and graceful.

The fourth pattern is a wonderful pair of drawstring pants. The pants can be worn loose and baggy or snug and sleek. You can combine the pants with the pullover pattern to create a comfortable jumpsuit. The pattern can be made in a shorter length and worn as knickers or cut floor length and much fuller to create a palazzo look.

EQUIPMENT

It probably won't be necessary to dash out and buy much equipment to create the patterns in this book. Most of the items mentioned in the following list will be found among your sewing supplies (Fig. 5). Search through your existing sewing equipment and use the things at hand. A roll of *pattern drafting paper* such as Pattern Tracing Cloth (Staple Sewing Aids Corporation), Do-Sew (a product of Stretch and Sew), Stacy's Tracer (Stacy Fabrics), or Pellon nonwoven bonded textiles will produce the most effective and permanent patterns. The final result can be tried on, altered easily, folded for storage, and pressed with a warm iron, if necessary.

Newsprint may be used, but the patterns won't be nearly as permanent. Newspaper has a tendency to tear after a few uses. Another option is *wrapping paper* (brown, white, or whatever you happen to own).

Two pens of contrasting color are important as one will be used to draw the lines on your pattern, the other should be used for written notations or corrections and changes. Ball-point, felt-tipped, or fabric marking pens all work well on nonwoven fabrics.

A *yardstick* or long straightedge will be needed for drawing pattern lines but you will also find a dressmaker's curve an asset. It provides a firm edge for drawing curves along the hemlines, armholes, etc.

A *tape measure* is important for accurate body measurements. Try to find one that does not stretch, such as a laminated vinyl/fabric tape.

You'll use an asortment of *pins*, such as silk pins and/or glass-headed pins. Extra-long quilting pins are definitely helpful.

Small *weights* come in handy for anchoring finished pattern pieces while cutting garments. These can be an assortment of mini beanbags, ashtrays, or cutlery that won't get in the way of the scissors.

A good pair of *scissors* is a must. There are many on the market but I would strongly recommend Gingher shears and scissors. Their quality is high, and they are always ready to give the finest performance.

GENERAL PATTERN INFORMATION

As you read through the pattern directions and other information, you will discover frequent use of the word "approximately." This is not due to my inability to decide on sizes or terms. Approximately is used to indicate that there is plenty of room for your personal interpretation. It means "You be the judge, you be the designer." When you read this term, feel free to make personal changes, stretch or shrink a pattern, change buttonhole placements, raise or lower a neckline, or just plain let your imagination run free.

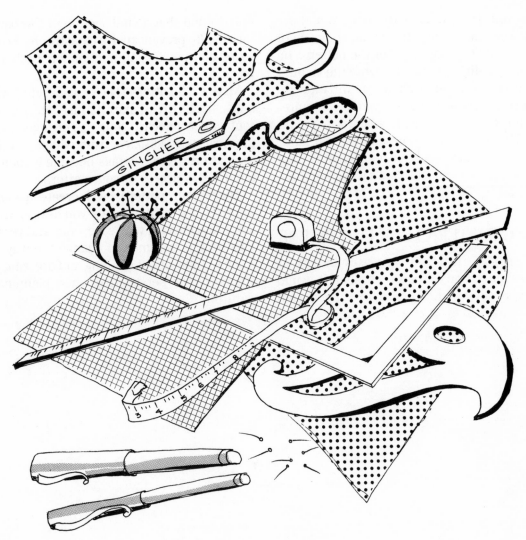

Fig. 5.   Equipment.

The basic patterns for the pullover and all other garments in this book are charted in a LARGE size. Measurements for MEDIUM and SMALL sizes are indicated in parentheses. If you wear a large size, use the first measurement given. Circle *all* the correct measurements for your size on each chart before you start to draft the patterns. This is the best way to prevent pattern errors. Use colored pen or pencil to make your measurements stand out on the page.

A ⅜″ seam allowance is included with each pattern, unless otherwise noted. This allowance is adequate for sewing with a conventional single-thread sewing machine or a 3- or 4-thread overlock sewing machine. These patterns are de-signed to be worn with a loose and easy, casual, fit. Pattern fitting lines will not be very critical so that you can be a little freer in your interpretations of each design.

Cut each basic pattern (your sloper) in as per-manent and sturdy a form as possible. Since there are many variations that you will make from the four original patterns, they will have to withstand considerable use. Nonwoven fabrics, muslin, or other inexpensive fabrics, which can be folded, unfolded, and ironed, altered, and stitched, will be usable for years and years. Avoid using tissue paper that can tear on first use and is generally perishable.

When you have completed a pattern and are ready to sew, take your patterns (and a pencil or pen) to the fabric shop. Lay out the patterns on fabric bolts of different widths. Write the amount of fabric required for each width variation directly on the pattern. Check yardage requirements for plaids and prints that have repeat motifs. This could save time, money, and labor during future sewing experiences. You won't have to rely on memory and guesswork when purchasing your fabric.

CODING PATTERNS FOR FUTURE USE

Unmarked pattern pieces can easily be lost or combined into a very strange garment. It would be horrid to set your heart on a particular design only to find that a vital section of the pattern is missing. To prevent such a catastrophe, be sure to write all specific information on each pattern piece.

Mark each pattern (FRONT, BACK, etc.) with the DATE, STYLE (dress, skirt, blouse, etc.), your current WEIGHT (in case your size changes), and the physical MEASUREMENTS from which you drafted the pattern. These details become a coding system foreasy access to your patterns.

These four patterns will create a complete wardrobe for whatever look you desire, whatever fabric you choose, with ease, chic, and versatility. This book is designed to change the way you've come to think about clothing and dressing and to broaden your perspective when planning your wardrobe.

MAKING A COMPLETE WARDROBE FROM 4 BASIC PATTERNS

Wardrobe Planning

Daily dressing doesn't have to be a traumatic event. Colors that match or blend, fabrics that work together, styles that flatter the figure and personality—these are the features we want to see when we open the closet door. A coordinated wardrobe is not beyond one's reach.

Looking over the past year's additions to your wardrobe, do you find that the colors and styles are within a similar range? Do your accessories in bright or contrasting colors blend with existing items as though they've always been there? We often lean towards a personal color scheme that results in instinctive wardrobing. In case the past year's additions don't work too well together, there are ways to revitalize your wardrobe.

A coordinated wardrobe does not have to be based on black, navy blue, dark brown, and beige. This was the basic color scheme worn by people in the retail trade of yore. You can certainly wear these colors if they enhance your hair and skin coloring, but there are many other options. Choose a primary color as a base for color planning: Red is not exactly a receding color, but if it happens to be a color you are fond of, use it as your basic color and coordinate around it. Use red with green (its complement) to tone it, with orange and pink to make it vibrate in summer, with a strong, deep blue (its primary color companion) for a crisp look all year around. Try burgundy accessories for a change of pace. Red combined with black and/or white will result in some striking effects. Red worn with khaki is a real knockout!

Many shops display coordinated fabric selections. Choices might include a print, several solids, and one or more stripes. These selections make wardrobing a snap! All the planning is done for you. You can sew coordinated separates by merely choosing from these fabrics on display. Most shops even supply a mirror for you to view the effect of these fabric combinations before you make your purchase. With clothing so well coordinated, accessories can blend with an entire wardrobe instead of being limited to one costume.

Fabric choices should suit your style of living. A meticulous person who feels uncomfortable with a rumpled look should avoid fabrics that wrinkle easily, such as linens or Indian cottons. If you are *very* particular about a fastidious appearance, choose fabrics with at least 50 percent polyester content to keep the finished garments as fresh and smooth as possible. If you are more trendy, you will be able to enjoy linens, cottons, and loosely woven natural fabrics.

Start with a plaid or print. Select solid colors for your coordinates that match the colors in the basic fabric. To add stripes to the group, look for colors in the stripes that match the solids you selected. The following pages illustrate a fully coordinated wardrobe you can make from patterns in this book.

START WITH A PLAID

• Choose a traditional Scottish tartan, say Black Watch. The colors of this plaid are forest green, navy blue, and red, possibly with a single or double thread of yellow woven through it. An unconstructed jacket and A-line dirndl skirt can be the foundation units of a completely coordinated wardrobe based on this tartan (Fig. 6).

• The same jacket pattern can be used for a second suit, with the skirt cut from the circle skirt pattern. The second jacket and skirt can be made in a solid forest green fabric (Fig. 7). The skirts and jackets are now interchangeable. You have four separate units that are usable with other items already in your closet.

Fig. 6.   Choose a Scottish tartan.   *Fig. 7.   Matching solids.*

• Add a culotte in navy blue. The culotte will go with the plaid jacket and blend nicely with the solid green jacket (Fig. 8).

• Continuing with additional separates is simple once you've gotten this far. You can add long pants in red or blue that pick up the narrow lines of the plaid (Fig. 9).

• If you have carefully saved the scraps from the above sewing, you no doubt have several large pieces that can now be put to good use. The shirt pattern (charted in the next chapter) has the type of styling that lends itself to a patchwork of fabric. Cut and pin the leftovers into sections for the shirt that will coordinate with all of the above garments.

You might have enough scraps to create more than one top. Woven fabric scraps will combine with outdated sweaters for an entirely new look and fabric extension (Fig. 8 and Fig. 9). If you

Fig. 8.   Add culotte and patchwork top.   Fig. 9.   Long pants and patchwork top.

have any difficulty planning the arrangement of the scrap fabric, do a tracing of the original top pattern as a sample; cut it apart in a pleasing spatial configuration. Decide which sections will have the patchwork and which sections will have the solid fabric pieces. The scrap sizes will determine the ultimate size of each section of your finished shirt. Pin the scrap pieces to the sample pattern. When you have a combination you like, pin the fabrics together and start to sew. Save the cut-up pattern for future use. Once you've made a patchwork top, you'll want another.

• Adding sweaters will extend your wardrobe: Choose a yellow, picked up from the plaid; a blue to match the culottes; a lighter value of the green used for the second suit; and a red to match the pants.

• To add stripes or prints to this wardrobe, try cotton shirting and silk crepe in any combination of the basic colors. These can make your wardrobe flexible for casual and dressy occasions, daytime and evening wear.

An unlined, unconstructed coat· can be worn over any of the above combinations. With the addition of a belt, it can also double as a dress.

Additional skirts, pants, and culottes can be planned in any of the colors and combinations already suggested. Try some tweeds with the plaids and solids; tweeds are versatile and can easily extend into new color groups.

START WITH A PRINT

Wool challis is a lovely, season-spanning fabric that can take up the slack during transitional times of the year. Challis is a soft, flowing fabric that can be dressed up or down. Choose a print in browns, taupe, burnt orange, and moss green, (typical colors for a redhead).

• Start your wardrobe by making a circle skirt and separate top from the challis print.

• Choose a soft silky fabric in a matte finish of moss green for an additional top and A-line skirt.

• A jacket and pants made up in taupe gabardine provides the crispness to complement the ensemble.

• Consider a burnt orange coat of nubby wool bouclé. You can edge-line the coat in the original challis print. This could then become a reversible garment, one that would pull the entire wardrobe together.

These styles, fabrics and colors all work well together. You can plump up the wardrobe with pullovers and cardigans; just pick up the colors in the original challis print. Add a few turtleneck T-shirts, and you have enough clothing to wear for any occasion, twelve months of the year.

Visit your local fabric shop with this new approach to wardrobe planning. You'll surely come up with lots of your own ideas. Just be careful not to go off on tangents if you're looking for maximum coordination with your existing separates. Don't get into color schemes that are really not for you.

As for the unconstructed look I've suggested, this refers to a soft garment, finished without any formal tailoring (often minus shoulder pads and facings). In short, it is a simple garment with a minimum of finishing details, often sewn completely by machine. Unconstructed clothes are easy as T-shirts to put together and just as comfortable to wear. Since all patterns in this book can be completed by this method, I would like to discuss it at this point.

An overlock machine (also known as a serger) will ease sewing by the unconstructed method. This is one of the most important pieces of equipment to be produced for home use (it was originally designed for commercial use but offered recently for the home market). A serger is a sewing machine that trims the seams as it overcasts the raw edge. It gives the finest finish anyone could ask for.

A serger practically eliminates the need for hand finishing. For example, hems and such can be exposed just as they come off the machine; no need to turn up a facing. Never again will you feel embarrassed by shaggy seams on the inside of your creations. Just run each section of a garment through the overlock machine and finish all raw edges before sewing an item together. Jacket collars won't need facings: A swish of the serger, and the collar edges are finished, the jacket completed. Because there is no bulk added by using an overlock machine, jackets and coats can be layered for warmth or fashion, one worn as a blouse or dress, the second as a jacket or topcoat. Collars will be compatible and the clothes interchangeable (Fig. 10).

Seam edges will be smooth as silk without seam binding. Seams can be sewn on the outside for a decorative effect—a real designer look. This method simplifies sewing to the point where an entire suit can be completed in two hours. If you don't already own a machine like this, check with a local distributor who may be able to give you a demonstration.

When you want fast and simple sewing, try the following method on your serger:

1. Cut the fronts, back, pockets, sleeves, and a single collar without a facing.

2. Finish the pockets on either the serger or a conventional sewing machine; then attach them to the fronts before any construction begins.

3. Sew the shoulder seams, connecting the fronts and back.

4. Attach the collar.

5. Set in the sleeves.

6. Close the side and sleeve seams in one continuous line of stitching, starting at the bottom edge of the jacket, sewing through the armscye (armhole) and down the length of the sleeve to the edge.

7. Sew completely around the outside of the jacket (including the collar) and finish the lower edges of each sleeve. The serger's stitching creates enough body around the outside edges for a garment to look very complete without any facings.

Fig. 10. Wear coat as dress.

21

Note: Without a serger, bind the raw edges of the jacket with foldover tape, or sew seams and topstitch to give the inside a nicely finished appearance. Your zigzag sewing machine probably has a serging stitch either built in or as a separate cam that will work passably. The only problem: Seams have a tendency to pucker when serged on a regular sewing machine. For edge-finishing on your regular sewing machine, use the proper foot, and stretch the fabric gently as you stitch to keep it flat and even. Try to maintain a constant, steady pressure on the treadle. Sew a line of straight stitching before serging the seams. Raw edges can also be overcast by using a conventional zig-zag stitch for the inside only, not as a decorative exterior finish.

Pullovers and Such:
From Shirts to Coats

Blouses, shirts, or pullovers create the aura for the skirts and pants we coordinate with them. These tops can transform casual separates into evening clothes and blend unrelated separates into a complete costume. This featured pullover (or pop-top) is that type of style: very fashionable, very easy to sew, very comfortable, and a joy to wear (Fig. 11).

Fig. 11. Basic pullover.

This is a pattern that will be used over and over again with a wide assortment of fabrics. When you do select your yardage, consider the purchase of a little extra for a matching skirt and/or a pair of pants to complete an ensemble of wardrobe extenders. Matching tops and bottoms worn together can take on the look of a one-piece dress or jumpsuit; as separates, they're available to mix and match (Fig. 12). Your versatile separates become a basic wardrobe for travel, business, or pleasure. The utility and wearability of these pieces can be extended with shirts and sweaters, and enhanced with small accessories that match or contrast with the clothing already in your wardrobe.

Fig. 12.   The "costume look."

THE BASIC PULLOVER PATTERN

The design includes a short, stand-up collar and a classic dropped shoulder, front and back yokes, and several logical places to include pockets. The full sleeves allow plenty of room for you to layer a sweater or additional shirt underneath the pullover on a chilly day. In fact, the loose sleeves and dropped shoulder line is as fashionable for active sportswear as it is for dressier clothes.

The length of this pullover can easily be adjusted to suit your height and preference, but consider the longer line shown in the sketch (Fig. 14). When worn as an overshirt, this length covers even your longest sweaters. The shirt's drawstring at the bottom allows you to vary the look by fitting it to your waistline or hips. Either line will give the body definition without detracting from the oversized look.

The drawstrings at the cuffs make the sleeve fit comfortably at the wrist or higher up the arm. Elastic of either ¼″ or ½″ can easily be substituted for the drawstrings. The same size casing can be used either way. This pattern evolves into a medley for your wardrobe: pullovers, dresses, evening gowns, jackets, coats, and an assortment of vests. Details for these variations follow the pattern-drafting directions.

Draft the body and yoke sections of the pattern in one piece; this provides a complete body for the pattern. You will be free to vary the position of the yoke, making it shorter or longer by merely folding the yoke line to a different depth. You will also be able to eliminate it completely by cutting the entire body of the shirt in one piece without having to pin the sections together or otherwise tamper with the lines of the pattern.

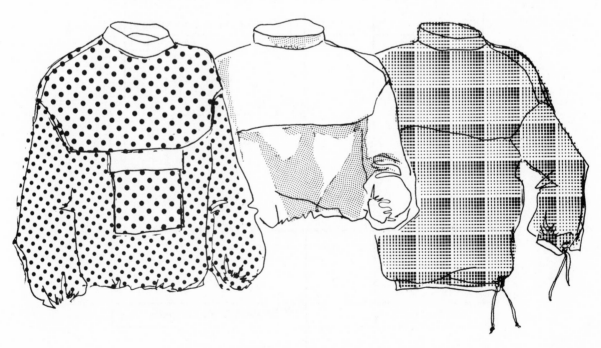

Fig. 13.   Change the fabric, change the style.

Draw the yoke line across the pattern pieces, front and back, as indicated in the diagrams. When adjusting the length of the yoke, be sure that any amount subtracted from the actual yoke section is added to the length of the body to retain the continuity of the design.

DRAFTING THE PATTERN

See "General Pattern Information" in the Introduction for pattern sizing.

Front. The overall dimensions for the body of the shirt measure approximately 28″ square. Find a sheet of pattern paper large enough to include the entire pattern piece (left and right halves of the pattern front). When using your pattern for plaids, repeat patterns, or leather, a complete pattern piece is vital (Fig. 14).

Draw a vertical line down the middle of the paper to designate the center front of the pattern (Fig. 15). Along this line, mark the following points:

1. Starting at the top of the paper, mark the point where the neckline opening and the height of the shoulder line meet.

2. Draw a dash across the center line 1½″ below the first mark for the drop or slope of the shoul-

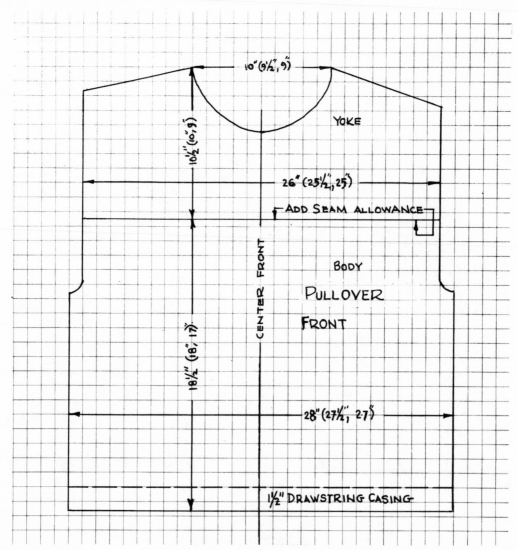

Fig. 14. Pullover pattern: front.

26

der line. This shaping allows the top of the shirt to lie smoothly across the shoulders but trims away some of the fabric bulk.

3. Measure down 4½″ (4″, 3½″) below the top of the shoulder line for the lowest point of the neckline curve.

4. The line for the yoke will be drawn 6″ (5½″, 5″) below the lowest point of the neckline curve. (10½″ [10″, 9½″] below the peak of the shoulder-neckline point)

5. From the line for the yoke, measure down 5″ (4½″, 4″) along the center line for the depth of the armhole. The yoke does not come completely to the bottom of the armscye. Too many seams meeting at this point would not only add bulk to the underarm, it would weaken the lower seam line of the armhole.

6. The bottom edge of the shirt is 13″ (12½″, 12″) below the lowest point of the armhole opening. Mark this point at the bottom of the center line.

7. Draw the line for the drawstring casing 1½″ below the hem fold.

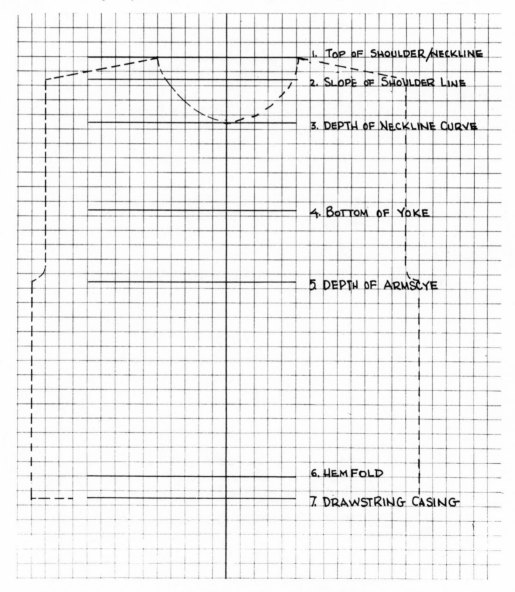

Fig. 15.   Measuring along center line: front.

Steps 1 to 7 are for the horizontal lines of your pattern. When these points are indicated along the center line, go on to the next series of measurements (Fig. 16). They are for the side seams (the width of the shirt). Don't attempt to complete any lines of the pattern until *all* the measurements are indicated on the pattern piece.

8. The neckline opening is 10″ (9½″, 9″) wide.

Indicate this measurement across the shoulder peak line.

9. The width across the shoulders is 26″ (25½″, 25″). Indicate half of this amount on either side of the center line along the shoulder-slope line.

10. Mark the depth of the neckline on the center line, 4½″ (4″, 3½″) below the shoulder peak.

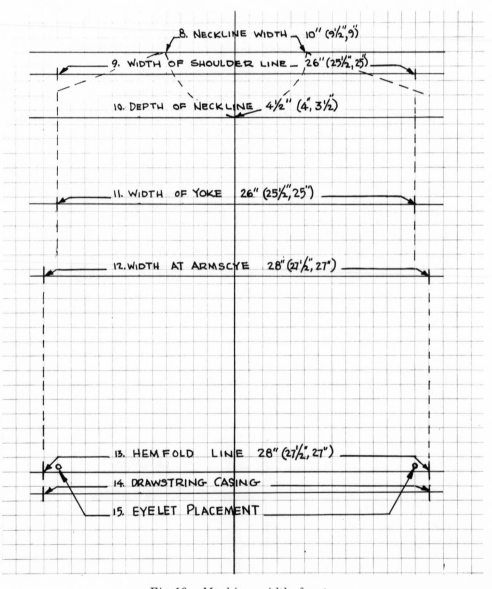

Fig. 16. Marking width: front.

11. Sketch the width across the yoke line: 26″ (25½″, 25″).

12. The width of the underarm is 28″ (27½″, 27″). Mark off half of this amount on each side of the center front line at the lowest point of the armhole opening. The 1″ projection of the armscye at each side will be curved into the body of the shirt to give a little shaping to the sleeve and armhole.

13. The width at the bottom of the shirt is 28″ (27½″, 27″). Draw this line across the bottom of the pattern where you indicated the hemline.

14. Add a second line 1½″ below the hem for the drawstring casing. The depth of the casing is adequate for any type of finish for this top (drawstring, elastic, or conventional hem) but you can vary the depth of the casing or hem, if you prefer. For a drawstring, 1½″ is adequate. This provides 1″ for the casing and ½″ seam allowance. When using elastic, this is the rule of thumb: Measure the width of the elastic plus ¼″ to ½″ seam allowance. If you are adding a trim at the bottom of the pattern and eliminating the casings, just substitute a simple seam allowance.

15. Indicate the location for the eyelets. Measure ¼″ up from the hem fold and 1″ in from the outside edge of the garment. Mark that point at either side of the shirt. The best eyelet is a metal grommet; it will withstand the maximum wear. Embroidered eyelets can be used if metal grommets aren't available.

You will now be able to complete the pattern FRONT by drawing the outside lines, connecting all of the measurements marked on the pattern paper:

• Draw the slanted line of the shoulders first. All the vertical lines of the pattern will hang from the outer points of the shoulders.

• Draw the line for the yoke completely across the pattern where indicated. Somewhere on the yoke line, write ADD SEAM ALLOWANCE or SEAM ALLOWANCES NOT INCLUDED. Seam allowances must be added to both the yoke and the body of the shirt when cutting the body of the shirt in two sections. (You wouldn't want the piece to be an inch too short to finish the shirt properly.)

• Complete the line of the armhole opening and the one-inch extension of the armscye at the base. Curve the corner where these lines meet.

• Connect the points of the side seam from the base of the armhole opening past the hemline, continuing down through the lower line of the casing.

Label the pattern: PULLOVER, FRONT, SIZE.

Back. The BACK section of the pattern can be traced from the FRONT with the exception of the neckline opening. At the front, the neckline drop is 4½″ (4″, 3½″) down from the topmost point of the center line. The neckline drop for the back of the pattern is 2″ below the top of the shoulder-neckline point. Simply trace all other lines from the front of the pattern and redraw the neckline curve. Just be sure to trace the yoke and the bottom lines for the drawstring casing as they appear on the pattern front. These lines do not change from front to back (Fig. 17).

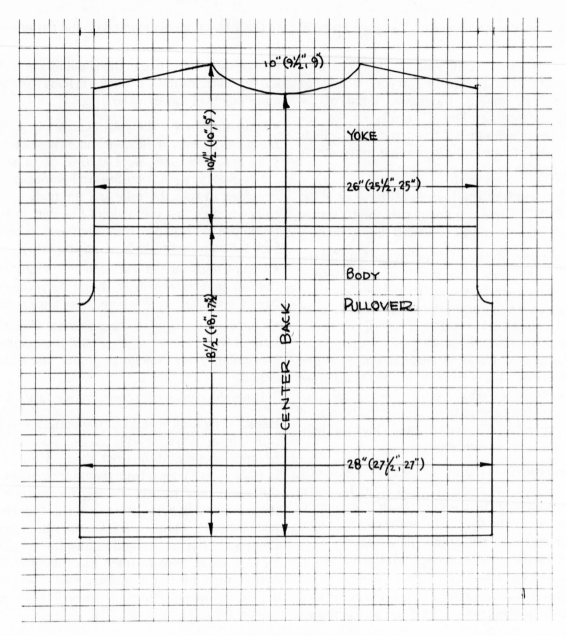

Fig. 17. Pullover pattern: back.

Sleeve. The general dimensions for the sleeve will require a piece of pattern paper approximately 26″ by 30″. The actual measurements of the sleeve are 22½″ long by 28″ wide (Fig. 18). Measure your sleeve length requirements by extending a tape measure from wristbone to wristbone acrss the back of your shoulder line. This will give you the actual measurement.

To ensure the proper amount for blousing of the sleeve, extend your arms straight out from your shoulders and measure the total length from wristbone to wristbone. Then pull your arms together, extending them straight out in front of you. Again measure from wristbone to wristbone across the high back. The difference between the two measurements will equal the amount of ease needed for the length of the sleeve. The pattern measures 71″ across the back of the shirt. Minus seam allowances and casings, there are 67″ for actual finished sleeve length. Be sure that this length is adequate for you; or make any necessary length corrections before you draft the sleeve pattern.

The sleeve has a slightly curved top that fits

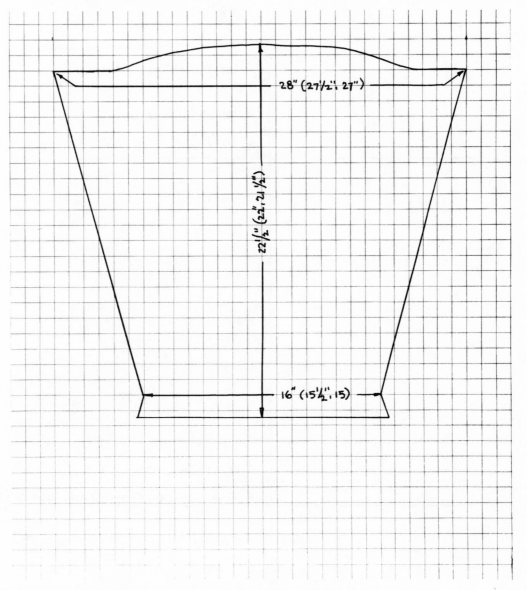

Fig. 18. Pullover pattern: sleeve.

smoothly into the armhole opening. Following are the dimensions to be marked on your pattern (Fig. 19).

1. Draw the center line for the sleeve.

2. Mark the topmost point of the sleeve.

3. Draw a dash 1½" below that point to designate the curve of the sleeve top.

4. The entire length of the sleeve is 22½" (22", 21½") to the hem from the topmost point.

5. Below the hemline, mark off an additional 1½" for the drawstring casing.

The following measurements are for the width of the sleeve (Fig. 20).

6. The measurement at the widest point of the

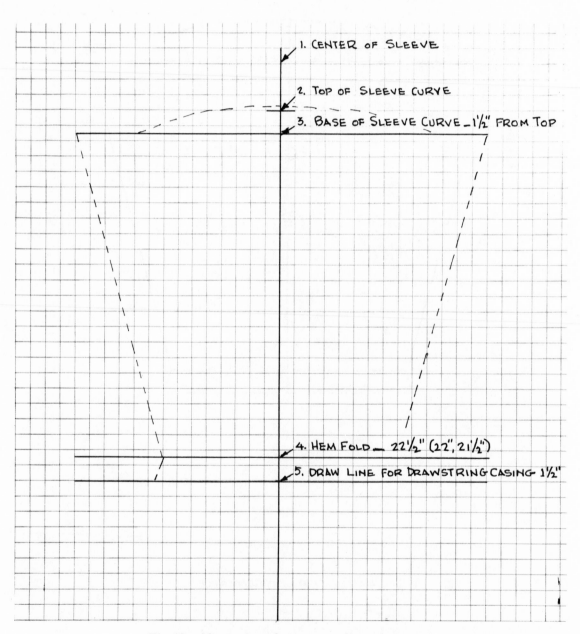

1. CENTER OF SLEEVE

2. TOP OF SLEEVE CURVE

3. BASE OF SLEEVE CURVE — 1½" FROM TOP

4. HEM FOLD — 22½" (22", 21½")

5. DRAW LINE FOR DRAWSTRING CASING 1½"

Fig. 19. Measuring along center line: sleeve.

sleeve, at the underarm is 28″ (27½″, 27″). Draw half of this measurement on either side of the center line at the second slash. When drawing the curve of the sleeve top, keep the first and last 2″ straight and continue across the center, drawing a gentle curve for the top of the sleeve.

7. The width at the hem of the sleeve is 16″ (15½″, 15″). Mark half of this width along the line at the bottom of the sleeve on each side of the center line.

8. Draw a second line 1½″ below the hem fold for the casing.

9. There are two eyelets inserted in the hemline of each sleeve to allow the drawstring to pull freely without fraying the fabric of the sleeve. These eyelets are placed ¼″ above the hemline fold at the outer edges of each sleeve.

Add a note on your pattern: SLEEVE (CUT 2).

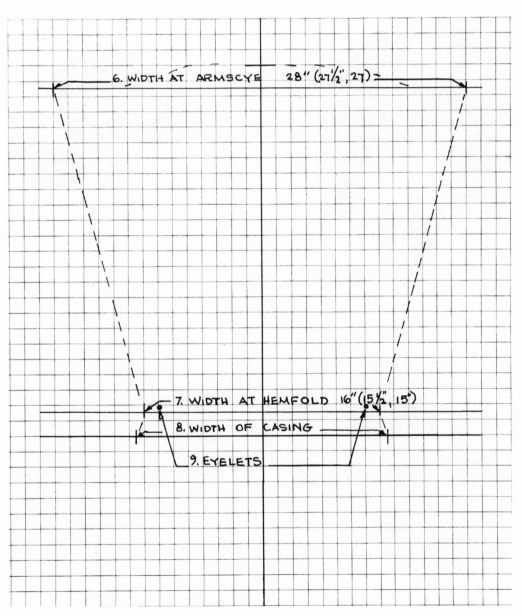

Fig. 20. Marking width: sleeve.

Collar. There are several different collar styles that would suit this versatile shirt: mock turtle, folded turtleneck, full cowl, etc. Keep in mind that whatever style you use, the opening should be wide enough to pull over your head.

1. The collar can be cut as a bias strip 25½″ long by 5½ to 6″ wide. This results in a wide turtleneck effect. When attached at the neckline of the shirt, it is folded in half and stitched. It is then folded down when worn (Fig. 21).

2. The collar can be cut as a straight strip 25½″ long by 3½″ wide. Cut this collar along the selvage. It is a short, stand-up collar that is sewn into a ring and should be interfaced for a firm finish (Fig. 22).

3. A cowl, cut long enough, can be pulled up over the head as a hood in inclement weather (Fig. 23 and Fig. 24). Cut the collar 25½″ wide by at least 16″ to 20″ deep. Hem one long edge; sew the opposite side around the neckline in a single thickness. Wear it casually scrunched down around the neck.

Fig. 21.   Wide turtleneck collar.

Fig. 22.   Stand-up collar.

Fig. 23.   Cowl collar.

Fig. 24.   Cowl collar worn as a hood.

There is no need for separate pattern pieces for these collars. Somewhere on the shirt pattern, write yourself a note, indicating the dimensions for each variation. To cut this collar on the straight of the goods, measure along the selvage. To cut the collar on the bias, fold the fabric on the *true bias* and cut the length and width you need.

SEWING METHODS: PULLOVERS

We all have our little tricks and techniques for putting a shirt together. Sometimes they work, sometimes they just give us headaches. The following is a very fast and efficient method that is based on the commercial method of garment construction. It is simple enough to cut your sewing time and help you forget how to spell "sewing headache." Follow this construction method whether your shirt has a separate yoke or a one-piece body.

1. Sew the front and back sections of the yoke together at the shoulder seams (Fig. 25).

2. Attach the collar to the yoke (or neckline of the shirt) at this point when there is the least amount of fabric to handle. Sew the bias strip into a ring (Fig. 26). To stitch the collar to the shirt there are two methods you can try:

• Pin the top edge of the collar ring around the neckline with right sides together and sew (Fig. 27). Turn up the raw edges of the collar and pin over the seam on the inside, folding the collar in half. Stitch in the original seam line, sewing around the entire collar (Fig. 28). Use caution—keep all edges smooth under the pressure foot. (You don't want this seam to pucker, gather, or pleat.)

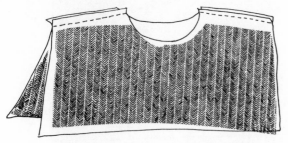

Fig. 25. Sewing the shoulders.

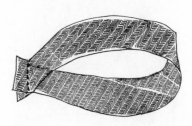

Fig. 26. Sewing the collar ring.

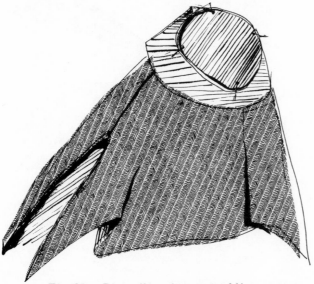

Fig. 27. Pin collar ring to neckline.

Fig. 28. Finishing collar.

• There is another method for attaching this type of collar. If you have an overlock machine, simply close the ends of the collar with right sides together and sew, forming a ring. Fold the collar ring down, matching the raw edges, right side out (Fig. 29). Pin the collar to the neck edge with the seam at the center back, inserting additional pins at both shoulder seams and the center front. Stitch around on the serger and your collar is completed. This method can also be used if you have a serging stitch with your regular sewing machine.

3. Sew the body to the yoke front and back, but do not complete the side seams (Fig. 30). The side seams and the sleeves will be completed later in one continuous line of stitching.

4. Pin the sleeves to the armhole. Stretch gently to shape as you sew. Keep the two sections (the body of the shirt and the sleeve) completely smooth and even. Topstitch along the seam, if desired.

5. When all sections of the shirt have been connected, sew the side seams from the bottom edge through the armscye and down the length of the sleeve (Fig. 31).

6. The metal eyelets for the sleeve and hemline drawstrings should be inserted before the hems are completed. If you did not mark the location for the grommets, they should be inserted at a point approximately ¾" on each side of the seam line, ¼" up from the hem fold at the bottom of

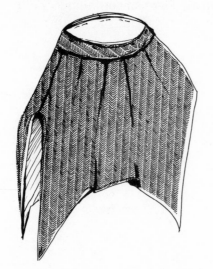

Fig. 29.   Collar: overlock method.

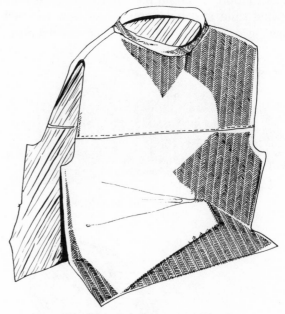

Fig. 30.   Sewing yoke to body.

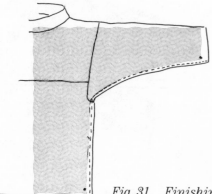

Fig. 31.   Finishing side seams and eyelets.

each sleeve. A machine-stitched eyelet can be substituted for a metal one, but the metal will hold up better under the constant rubbing of the drawstring. Repeat at the hem of the shirt. Be sure to reinforce the area for the eyelets with a small piece of fabric or interfacing on the underside to prevent them from tearing out of the fabric.

7. Turn up the casings along the hemlines of both sleeves and body of the shirt; then stitch.

Shoelaces or ribbon can be used for drawstrings; or make your own from matching fabric. Drawstrings for the sleeves should be long enough to go completely around the wrist plus enough length to tie, approximately 14″ to 16″. The bottom of the shirt calls for two strings, two strips of fabric, 30″ long by 1½″ wide, long enough to prevent the ends from slipping back into the casing when the ends are untied.

Fold each strip in half lengthwise, right sides together, and stitch ¼″ in from the unfinished or raw edge (Fig. 32). Turn each string to the right side. Thread through the casings and tie a knot at each end to keep the strings from slipping back into the casings. You can cinch up the strings to make the lower band fit around your waistline or allow the shirt to hang loosely below your hips—

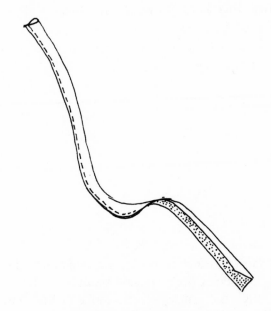

Fig. 32. Drawstrings.

either way looks great. Wear it over a blouse, sweater, or dickey. Don a pair of pants or an evening skirt of ankle or floor length and your pullover will be *the* finishing touch. Enjoy it with your favorite culottes or cropped pants. Each combination you wear will feel new and exciting.

POCKETS

INSEAM POCKETS

Inseam pockets are a nice addition to this shirt. Sew them on during the construction, before the side seams are closed.

1. Each pocket will require a 12-inch square of fabric.

2. Mark the shirt at each side seam for the location of the pockets. Pin pocket sections to the *front*.

3. With right sides together, sew the pocket to the shirt front between the marks (Fig. 33).

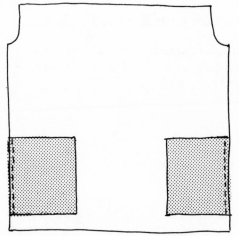

Fig. 33. Attaching pocket sections.

4. Sew the opposite edge to the back (with right sides together) between the marked points (Fig. 34).

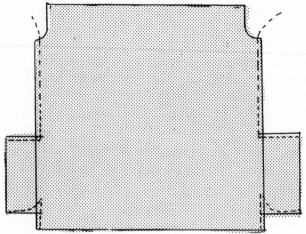

Fig. 34.   *Sew pockets to opposite sides.*

5. Turn the shirt to the wrong side and fold the pockets flat. Stitch the side seam from the hem through the armscye to the edge of the sleeve, following the pocket contour shown (Fig. 35).

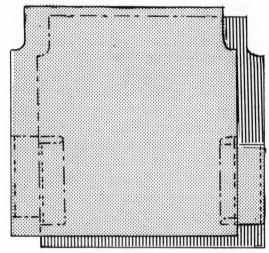

Fig. 35.   *Closing side seams and pockets.*

6. Finish the other side to correspond.

7. Turn shirt to right side and stitch-in-the-ditch at each side to secure the lower seam of each pocket (Fig. 36).

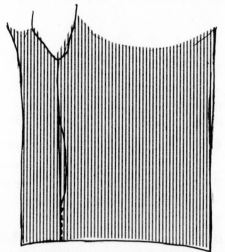

Fig. 36.   *Finishing detail: inseam pockets.*

KANGAROO POCKETS

A kangaroo pocket is another pocket variation that comes up often in my suggestions. I find their size and location most practical. Kangaroo pockets combine with so many styles; they can even be added to the sweat shirts, robes, or other items of clothing you already have in your wardrobe.

1. Cut two 12″ squares of fabric (Fig. 37).

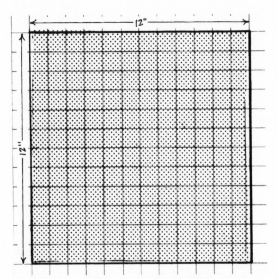

Fig. 37. Kangaroo pockets: Cut fabric squares.

2. With right sides together, stitch around the outside edges, leaving a 2″ opening at the bottom to reverse the pouch (Fig. 38).

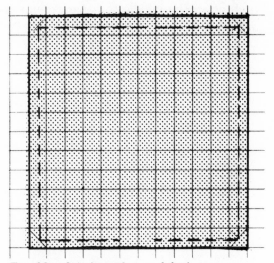

Fig. 38. Stitch pocket and facing.

3. Turn to the right side. Topstitch completely around the pocket, closing the turning slot (Fig. 39).

4. Pin the pocket to the shirt, centering 1″ under the yoke seam. If your shirt has no yoke, center the pocket 7″ below the lowest point of the neckline curve.

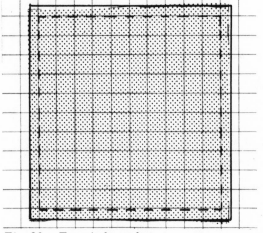

Fig. 39. Topstitch pocket.

5. Sew around the pocket, as shown in the illustration, backtacking or bartacking at the end of each seam to prevent the pocket from tearing away from the shirt (Fig. 40).

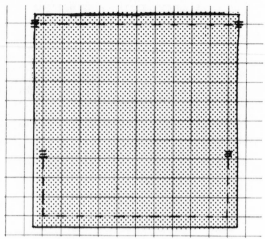

Fig. 40. *Attach pocket to shirt.*

6. Stitch down the middle to separate into two pockets (Fig. 41).

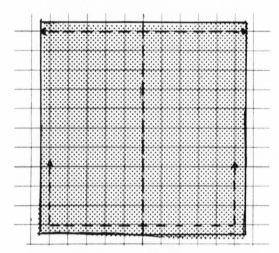

Fig. 41. *Finishing detail: kangaroo pocket.*

POUCH POCKETS

The same dimensions used for the kangaroo pockets (above) will yield pouch pockets with a flap.

1. Cut two 12″ squares of fabric and follow steps 1 through 3 given with kangaroo pockets. Sew the sections together and turn.

2. For the flap, you will need two rectangles, each 4″ high by 12″ wide (Fig. 42).

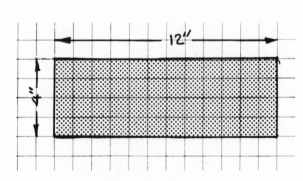

Fig. 42. *Pattern: pocket flap.*

3. With right sides together, sew the flap sections along three sides, leaving one long side open. Clip the corner point and turn the flap. Topstitch around the three seamed sides (Fig. 43).

4. Before you sew the body and yoke of the shirt together, center the pocket on the body section of the shirt from 1″ to 1½″ below the yoke seam. Stitch the pocket to the body section. Without a separate yoke, the pouch pocket is centered approximately 7″ below the neckline drop.

5. Center the flap over the pocket at the seam line. Pin the yoke and body together, sandwiching the raw edge of the flap between the yoke and body sections of the shirt front. Sew the yoke seam (Fig. 44).

6. Turn to the right side and topstitch along the yoke seam.

Velcro fastening tape or grip fasteners can be used to hold the flap down and close the pocket.

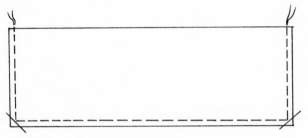

Fig. 43.   *Stitch pocket flap.*

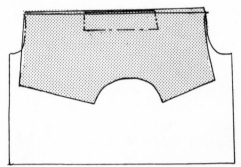

Fig. 44.   *Sew flap between body and yoke.*

PULLOVERS: MORE VARIATIONS

• Make this pullover from wool flannel, gabardine, or crepe. While taming some cold weather, this style could also be serviceable for most of the year. A pullover jacket, for instance, makes separates into a suit that can be worn from the office to social events with no effort. Inseam pockets on each side are handy additions, especially if you don't always carry a purse.

• Make the top in nylon ripstop for a water-repellent windbreaker. With matching pants, it will protect your golf and tennis clothes or keep you warm and dry when you jog (Fig. 45). A pocket, inserted at the yoke line of the center front, will hold everything you need.

• Sew the same outfit in corduroy. This fabric is certainly a season spanner and can add a little dressier note to your sportswear. Look for some of the more decorative finishes currently being used on this old standby.

• For summer wear or tropical vacations, cotton gauze is the answer. Because of its easy care and extensive color range, cotton gauze has become a very popular fabric. The loose weave lets the breezes cool you while the cotton—that wonderful, natural fibre—protects you from the sun (Fig. 46). This inexpensive fabric can help you fill out your summer wardrobe, adding color for any occasion.

• Cut this style from chiffon or lace for a dressy top (Fig. 47). It will revitalize last year's camisole or sleeveless blouse with matching pants or skirt. The same sheer top over a spaghetti-strapped dress can provide a whole new look for a fashion that may have been in your closet for several seasons.

• Don't overlook crinkled or wrinkled silk. With this new version of what was once considered a delicate fabric, you'll no longer object to silk be-

Fig. 46.   Summer cooler.

Fig. 45.   Active sportsuit.

Fig. 47.   Lace overblouse.

cause it wrinkles easily. The crinkle finish adds a whole new world of practicality to this ancient fabric. Available in a rainbow of beautiful colors, crinkled silk lends itself to this pullover or any of the patterns in this book.

• The low yoke of this shirt provides a perfect space to add decorative details. Instead of sewing the pocket flap into the yoke seam, pin it directly under the yoke line; center it above the pocket and stitch in place (Fig. 48).

A section of patchwork created from fabric scraps could easily be used for the yoke (Fig. 49).

The result is a striking top that can match a multitude of pants and skirts to create a series of complete ensembles.

• You can use the decorative cams that came with your sewing machine to produce beautifully embroidered fabric. Use the machine-embroidered fabric for the yoke, body, or sleeves of this pullover (Fig. 50). Just select the patterns to be embroidered, and choose the thread that coordinates with the majority of garments in your wardrobe. For more professional results, embroider the fabric before you cut the pattern.

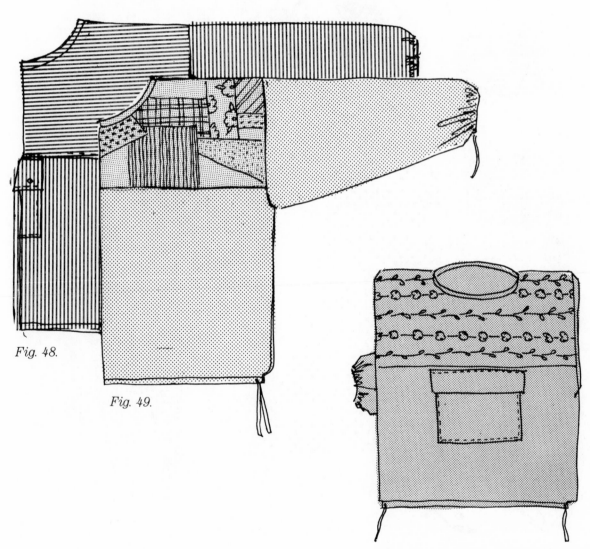

Fig. 48.

Fig. 49.

Fig. 50.   Embroidered inserts.

43

FINISHING TOUCHES

The following suggestions are just a few of the details that can turn simple separates into elegant costumes—the finishing touches that create a personal wardrobe. Change the entire appearance of the pullover with some simple variations (handled without actual pattern changes): Alter the width of the shirt and pleat the excess fabric to fit the yoke. Extend the length and wear with slim pants. Change the collar and/or neckline and you have again revised

Fig. 51. Variations without pattern changes.

its appearance without making any changes in the original basic pattern. Each result will be new and fresh (Fig. 51).

• If you prefer a collarless top, substitute a bias binding or foldover braid around the neckline edge. To prevent the neckline from sagging, shorten the depth of the front to 3½″.

• Or you can finish this shirt with ribbing around the neckline, bottom edges of the sleeves, and hemline (Fig. 52). Ribbing adds a handsome sweat-shirt touch that can be casual or dressy. Readily available, ribbing can be purchased by the yard at most fabric shops. Use this rule of thumb for measuring:

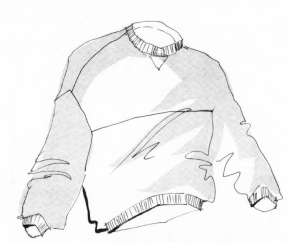

Fig. 52. Pullover with sweatshirt styling.

☐ **Neckline**: Subtract 2″ to 3″ from the actual measurement.

☐ **Waistline**: Subtract 3″ to 4″ from the actual measurement.

☐ **Wrist**: Use the actual measurement.

The shirt can be cut from knitted or woven fabrics without pattern adjustments and then finished with matching or contrasting rib-knit trim. Used with woven fabrics—the contrast between these textures is very handsome.

• If you're looking for something luxe, try ruffles at the bottom of each sleeve and around the neckline. At the wrists, elastic will be a better choice for the casings than drawstrings (Fig. 53). Bias strips, 3″ wide, cut from matching fabric or

ruffled eyelet trim in a matching or contrasting color, will work beautifully. A double row of ruffling around the neckline will add a feminine touch near the face. Band the opening for a drawstring casing to make the neckline a little more adjustable. To plan a nice ruffle, cut the strips approximately 1½ times the measurement of the space to be covered. For example, a 10″ wide sleeve edge requires a 15″ to 20″ strip for enough wrist flounce; a 28″ neckline opening could use 42″ to 56″ of ruffling.

Fig. 53. Pullover with ruffled trim.

CONVERTING THE PULLOVER:
OPEN-FRONT SHIRT

This pullover pattern can easily be converted to a shirt that opens in front. There are no pattern changes to make. Any alterations can be done during the layout and cutting of the new shirt.

1. Fold the pattern vertically along the center front line (Fig. 54). Since the shirt will open at the front, this part of the pattern will be cut in two pieces.

2. Place the pattern piece on the folded fabric, leaving 3″ at the selvage side for the front bands (Fig. 55). These can either be cut in one piece with the fronts or cut as separate pieces. Either way, the front bands will need interfacing.

3. Since this shirt will not pull over the head, the neckline can be narrowed, the collar snugged closer to the neck. Cut 1½″ inside the pattern line around the neck opening, narrowing it to 7″ of width, 3″ of front drop. Follow the contours of the pattern (Fig. 56).

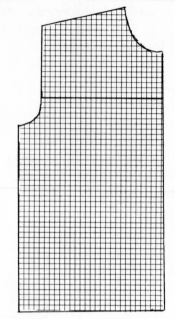

Fig. 55. Pattern layout: open-front shirt.

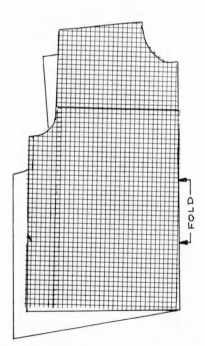

Fig. 54. Fold pattern for open-front shirt.

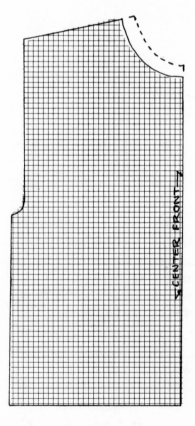

Fig. 56.
Adjusting
neckline.

4. Cut the back section of the pattern as drafted with the exception of the neckline. This is shortened 1½″ as was the front.

5. There are no changes for the sleeves.

6. The collar is a straight strip of fabric 16″ long by 6″ wide. It, too, will need interfacing.

SEWING METHODS: OPEN-FRONT SHIRT

Attach the breast pockets to the front sections of the shirt before the actual construction begins. Then assemble the shirt by the commercial method: Sew the shoulder seams, collar, sleeves, and side seams; then assemble the front band, and complete all the hems.

There was once a time when the left or right overlap of the buttonholes designated whether the shirt or jacket was for a man or a woman. Unisex dressing has changed all that. Today you decide which side is more *comfortable* for buttoning and that determines whether the buttonholes go on the left or right.

• To prepare the shirt for buttonholes, pin and sew a separate, interfaced buttonhole band along the front edge; the right side of the band faces the wrong side of the shirt (Fig. 57). Fold a narrow hem along the raw edge and turn the band to the right side of the shirt. Topstitch close to the seam edge. Sew again along the folded edge of the band and topstitch, catching the folded edge as you sew (Fig. 58). Mark the band for 7 evenly spaced buttonholes, ½″ from the edge of the tab, 3″ to 3½″ apart.

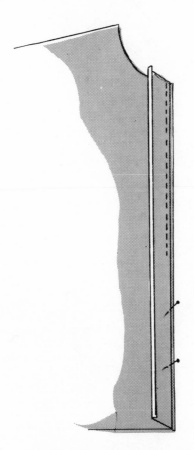

Fig. 57. Attaching front band: open-front shirt.

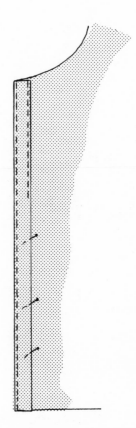

Fig. 58. Finishing front band: open-front shirt.

The opposite front edge can either be finished with a tab or just a simple facing. To face the button side, interface the band and sew it to the shirt, right sides of fabric together. Turn the band to the wrong side and fold under a narrow hem at the raw edge. Topstitch ⅛″ inside the folded edge, catching the hem as you secure the tab. Mark the buttons to correspond with the buttonholes.

• If the fabric is the same on both sides (double faced), the band and facing can be cut with the body of the shirt in one piece. Put the interfacing for the band on the top side. Fold over a narrow hem along the raw edge and press the entire band over the front of the shirt. Stitch along the outside edge; then stitch along the inside edge, catching the folded hem as you sew. Mark the band for 7 buttonholes, as detailed above.

Complete the facing on the opposite side. (See the details for preparing a separate, interfaced buttonhole band at the beginning of this discussion on buttonholes.)

You can wear this shirt tucked into a waistband, loose (as a smock top), or belted. It can also serve as a lightweight jacket over a tank top, T-shirt, or blouse (Fig. 59).

Well, now you've made your shirt and you're happy with it. You've even tried some variations on the original pattern. But what can you do with that pattern besides folding it neatly and stowing it in a drawer? Use your pattern to make a coat— a coat that would be as comfortable as the shirt you've just completed.

Fig. 59. Open-front shirt.

COATS

Coats come in a wonderful variety of lengths (Fig. 60). Most of these coats have names: jacket, car coat, seven-eighths, knee length, skirt length, shinbone, or formal (which moves the hemline to the floor).

A shinbone-length coat is handsome in combination with a pair of matching pants (and pants suits are always in style). If you have enough fabric to make a matching skirt, so much the better. The suit can then be worn two ways, and the coat can also be worn over other outfits. You can cut the entire coat from the back, front, and sleeve sections of the pullover pattern.

Fig. 60.   Coat and jacket styles.

BACK

Begin with the back pattern. The only change that must be made is the length for the planned coat. Decide how long you want it to be. (A full length coat should hang approximately 1″ to 2″ below your skirt hem. All other variations are up to you.)

Any changes you make will be on the fabric, not on the pattern. Place the pattern on the fabric. Stretch your tape measure to the desired length and mark that point on your fabric with pins, a bit of soap, or tailor's chalk (Fig. 61).

Cut the yoke and body separately, adding a seam allowance at the bottom edge of the yoke and along the top of the body section. When using a separate yoke, keep in mind that a finished garment is always more handsome when the details used on the front of the garment are carried around to the back, keeping the design continuity of that item.

To eliminate the yoke, the back and front sections can be cut in one piece. The lines of the coat will be a bit simpler and you can sew it together a little faster.

The width of the fabric will determine whether or not a center back seam is necessary. If the fabric is too narrow to accommodate the entire width of the pattern's back, use this procedure: Fold the back section of the pullover pattern in half lengthwise. Cut the back in two sections, adding a seam allowance at the center back for each side. (Be sure to reverse the pattern as you cut the left and right halves for the coat back.)

Lay the pattern on the fabric. Measure down from the hemline of your pattern to the point where the new hem for the coat will be. Cut straight down the sides, outside the seam allowance, to below the hem allowance at the bottom. Cut straight across the lower edge.

FRONT

The front of the coat will be cut in two sections, left and right. Fold the pattern front section in half lengthwise, along the center front line. Allow an additional 1½″ at the center front edge; place the pattern at this point, parallel to the selvages of the folded fabric (Fig. 62). This allowance will provide a little extra room for a faced tab for buttons and buttonholes at either side of the front or a little overlap for an unstructured coat without closures.

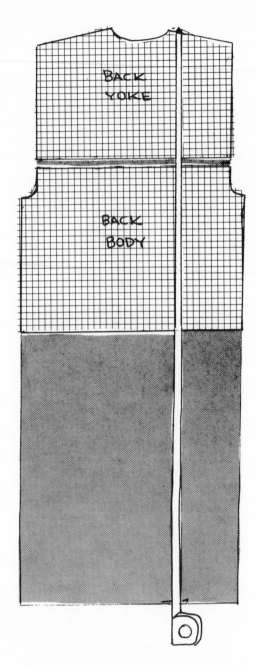

Fig. 61. Mark fabric for coat length.

Mark off the yoke section, adding a seam allowance at the bottom. Pockets and flaps can be inserted into this seam line of the yoke on the front.

FACINGS

Shaped facings can be cut in one piece (with the body of the coat) rather than cut and stitched on separately. To cut facings in one piece with the coat, extend the fronts 2½″ to 3″ plus the curved neckline extension—a total of at least 3″ to 4″ additional fabric at the center front edges. Curve the neckline for the facing to correspond to the curve of the neckline of the front section of the pattern, extending the end to meet the shoulder seam (Fig. 63).

The front facings can be cut separately. Lay the pattern piece on pattern drafting paper. Copy the shape of the neckline, extending this line out 1½″ beyond the center front line to allow a little extra width at the front for overlap and seam allowances (Fig. 64). Continue down the front, cut-

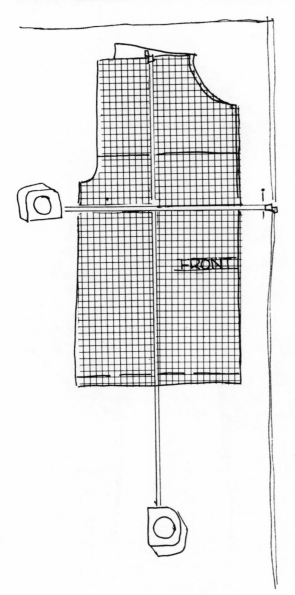

Fig. 62. Allowance for facings.

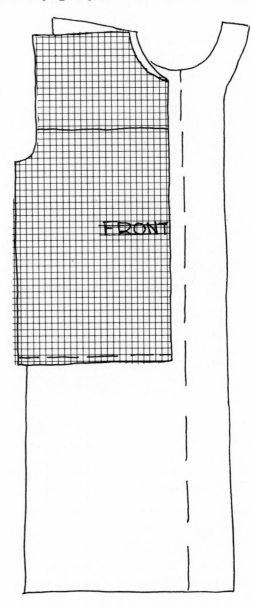

Fig. 63. Attached shaped facings.

ting the facings to the length you've chosen for the coat. Remember to add the seam allowance at the bottom.

Mark the fronts for the location of the buttons and buttonholes. Choose a pocket style and mark the coat for pocket locations. (See the Index for pocket style suggestions.)

SLEEVES

Cut two sleeves from the original pattern with no changes. Also, cut two straps to belt the lower part of the sleeve. It makes a much nicer finish than trying to add elastic to the hemline of a bulky fabric.

POCKETS

The coat illustrated (Fig. 65) has two oversized patch pockets. These pockets are 13″ wide by 14″ high. You can either cut four sections (two pockets and two facings), or just cut two pockets from the coating and the facings from lining or

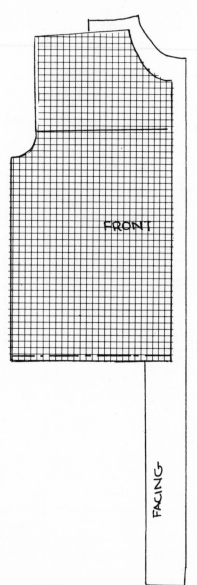

Fig. 64. Separate facings.

Fig. 65. Coat with funnel collar.

other fabric. There are many pocket variations that lend themselves gracefully to this style of coat.

To put flaps on these patch pockets, cut four pieces of fabric, each 13″ by 4″. See the section on pocket styles in this chapter for detailed instructions.

FUNNEL COLLAR

A funnel collar would be perfect for the design of this coat (Fig. 65). The neckline dips in front, allowing space for the shaping of the collar, with no additional changes necessary to the body of the coat.

To draft a pattern for the funnel collar, use a piece of pattern paper, approximately 10″ by 15″. Draw a vertical line at the left near the edge. Center and mark off 4″ across this line. This spot indicates both the center back and the fold line when you cut the funnel collar (Fig. 66).

Draw a line 10¾″ long, perpendicular to the original line, centered between the 4″. At the 10¾-inch point, mark a dot 3″ above the horizontal line. Extend and mark a second dot an additional 3¼″ out to the right. Curve the upper edge gently between the height at the center back and the 10¾-inch point near the center front or right edge of the collar. Extend the line across between the first and second dots.

Measure and mark a point 4″ below the line. Curve the bottom edge to connect the two dots. On the collar piece write: FUNNEL COLLAR, CUT 2, and INTERFACE.

To close this funnel collar, use either buttons or grip fasteners to match the coat closures.

SEWING METHODS: UNCONSTRUCTED COAT

This is an unlined coat. Finish all inside seam edges either on an overlock machine or with some form of seam tape before starting actual construction.

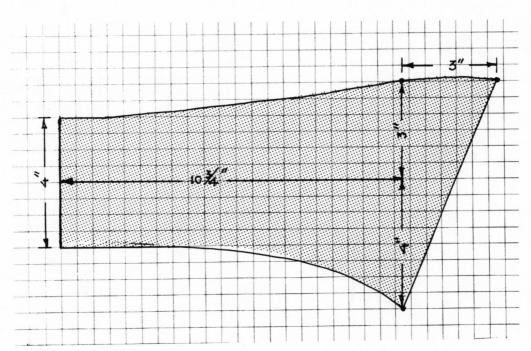

Fig. 66.   Pattern for funnel collar.

1. Sew the patch pockets to the two fronts of the body of the coat within the markings (Fig. 67).

2. Stitch the shoulder seams of the yoke and topstitch parallel to the seam line (Fig. 68).

3. Attach the body sections to the yoke, both front and back, leaving the side seams open. Top-stitch lower edge of the yoke (Fig. 69).

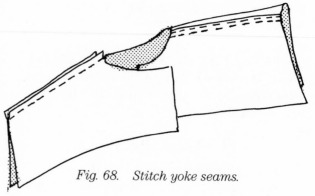

Fig. 68.   Stitch yoke seams.

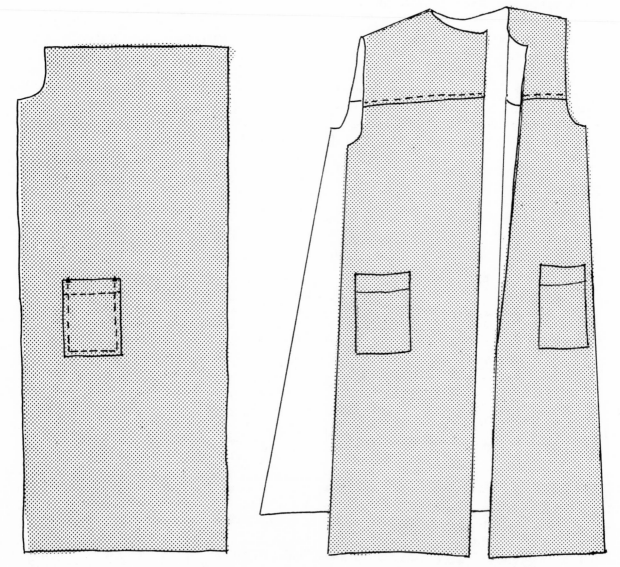

Fig. 67.   Sew pockets to front sections.

Fig. 69.   Attach body to yoke.

4. If you have cut separate facings, sew them to the center fronts. When sewing with lightweight fabrics, the facings should be interfaced before attaching to front edge. Iron-on interfacing may be used (Fig. 70).

5. Pin the collar around the neckline at several points—center back, both fronts, and the shoulder seams. Start from the center back. The measurement provides for a little lapel. Fold facings under and sew collar to neck edge (Fig. 71).

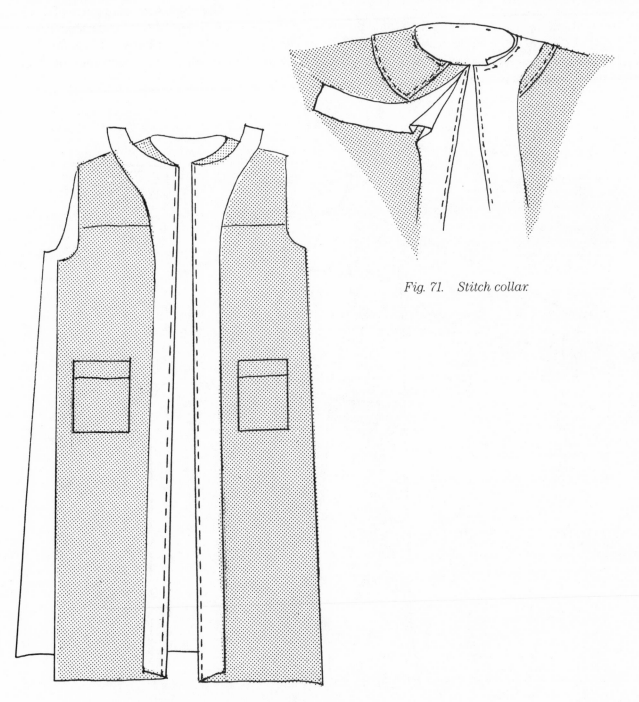

Fig. 71. Stitch collar.

Fig. 70. Stitch facings to fronts.

6. Attach sleeves to yoke; then topstitch (Fig. 72).

7. Starting at the bottom edge of the coat, sew the side seams together from the hem, through the armscye, to the bottom edge of the sleeve.

8. Complete wrist straps and belt, adding buckles or D-rings at one end of each strap (Fig. 73). Buckles can be eliminated by simply knotting the ends of the bands to secure them.

9. Pin the wrist straps to the sleeve at the seam line, approximately 3″ above the end of the sleeve.

If you are not planning closures for this coat, consider one snap or toggle at the top of the yoke near the collar. It would just keep the coat together on a windy day. Use a small piece of fabric or interfacing to underline the toggle at each side.

Your finished coat can be weatherproofed by your dry cleaner to give it a certain amount of soil as well as water resistance.

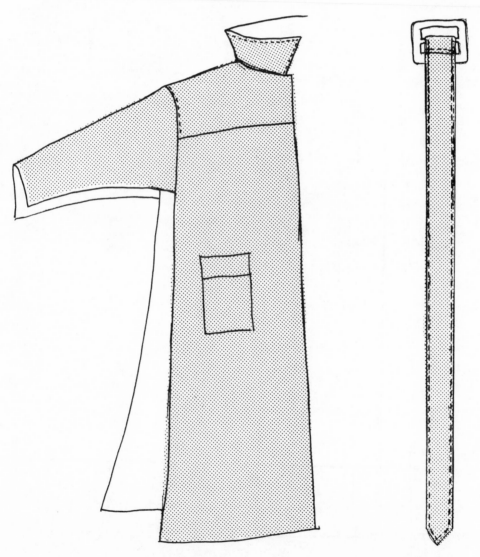

Fig. 72. Attach sleeves.   *Fig. 73. Belt and sleeve straps.*

WRAP COAT

A wrap coat should have enough fabric allowance added to the front to provide an adequate overlap (Fig. 74). Usually 6″ to 8″ is enough. Follow the neckline curve for your extensions (Fig. 75). The front facings should be wide enough at the upper edge to show a finished face when opened. When you want to close the coat all the way up to the neck, the opposing flaps will fit together nicely. Add a small button and buttonhole to secure the collar (Fig. 76).

Make a matching belt in your choice of styles. You can eliminate the collar and use a straight band of fabric around the neckline (Fig. 77).

Fig. 75.   Facing: wrap coat.

Fig. 77.   Wrap coat with banded neckline.

Fig. 74.   Wrap coat.

Fig. 76.   Neckline closure.

SWINGBACK COAT

The pullover pattern can be used for a swingback (bias back) coat—a graceful silhouette that will flatter most figures (Fig. 78). A short person should use caution in drafting this pattern. Pay careful attention to the scale of the coat. A very full swingback coat can make a short person appear to be standing in a hole! The only way to escape this image and still wear the style is to scale it to your stature. The coat should not be cut too full or too long. Instead of swinging the pattern two or more inches off the center line, try moving it one inch.

Cut the fronts on the lengthwise grain of the fabric, the same as for the conventional coat described earlier in this chapter. This creates a nice sweep of fabric, keeping the fullness in back and the fronts more slender and relatively straight. This style is flattering to all figure types. A complete description of the technique follows.

Fig. 78. Swingback coat.

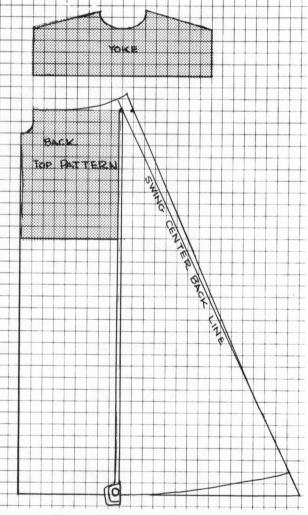

Fig. 79. Chart: Two-piece coat back.

BACK

Two-Piece Back. Cut the yoke separately, using the pattern piece as drafted (Fig. 79). The lower back or body can be cut in two sections (with a center back seam where you add the bias extension). The extra fullness in this wide sweeping back could add as much as 8″ to the lower edge of the back section, or as much as the fabric width will allow.

1. Cut the yoke and set it aside.

2. Fold down the yoke portion of the pattern to get it out of the way; then fold the *back* in half lengthwise. Place the pattern piece on the lengthwise grain of the fabric, allowing enough room at the bottom to include the new hem length (Fig. 80). Be sure you reverse the pattern piece to create a left and right section for the back, if you are not cutting on the fold.

3. To retain all the fullness at the center back, cut the side seams straight down from the armscye to the new hemline. Place the pattern with the armhole side or outside seam edge close to the selvage. Mark the new hemline with a few pins. Allow enough fabric at the bottom to include the hem facing (Fig. 81).

4. Mark the hemline across the entire width of the fabric and cut across the upper seam line, including a seam allowance at the top.

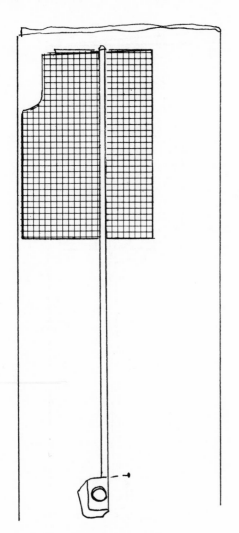

Fig. 80.   Measure length.

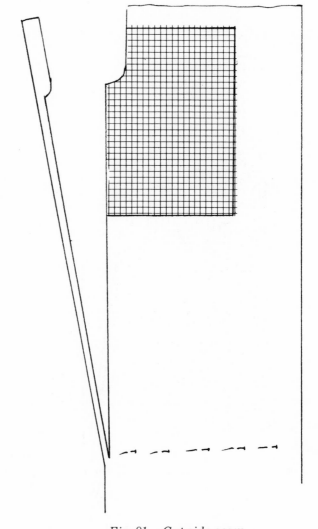

Fig. 81.   Cut side seam.

5. Now, swing the entire pattern piece off the center line to create a partial bias line for the center back of the coat. If you prefer *not* to move the pattern, use a straightedge as a guide from the uppermost point of the center back to the center back of the new hemline; cut along the angle indicated by your guide (Fig. 82). Complete the bottom edge by cutting along the line of pins or other markings.

One-Piece Back. You can cut the lower back of the coat in one piece and still provide bias fullness at the hemline. To begin, place the fold of the center back near the folded edge of the fabric, approximately 3″ from the top of the fabric (Fig. 83).

1. Mark the hemline and cut approximately one-third of the top seam line, starting from the folded edge of the fabric (Fig. 84).

2. Swing the pattern towards the selvage as much as the fabric width allows. Be sure that there is enough room at the bottom for the entire width of the hem and facing (Fig. 85).

3. Curve the cutting line for the upper edge just enough to blend the angle created by the top

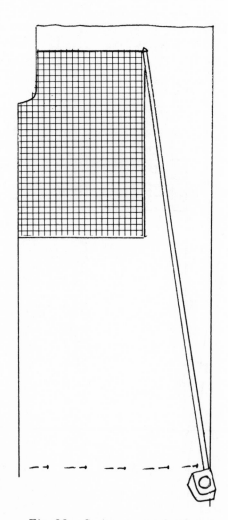

Fig. 82.   Swing center back.

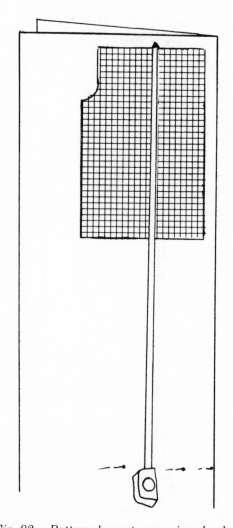

Fig. 83.   Pattern layout: one-piece back.

edge when you swing the pattern out from its original position.

4. Measure to be sure the length will be the same for both the front and back and that the two sections will fit together properly. To do this, drop a tape measure from the armhole to the new hem length at the side seam.

FRONT

1. Fold the FRONT section of the pattern in half along the center front line.

2. Lay the FRONT pattern piece on the folded fabric with the center front parallel to the selvage. Allow 2″ at the front edge for overlap or a facing and 2″ to 2½″ at the top for the curve of the top edge of the pattern piece (Fig. 86).

3. Cut the center front edges on the straight of the fabric from the neckline to the new hemline to keep the closures hanging in a straight line.

4. For the side seams, swing the pattern the same as for the BACK in step 2. Follow the directions in step 3 (BACK) for curving the upper line of the pattern piece.

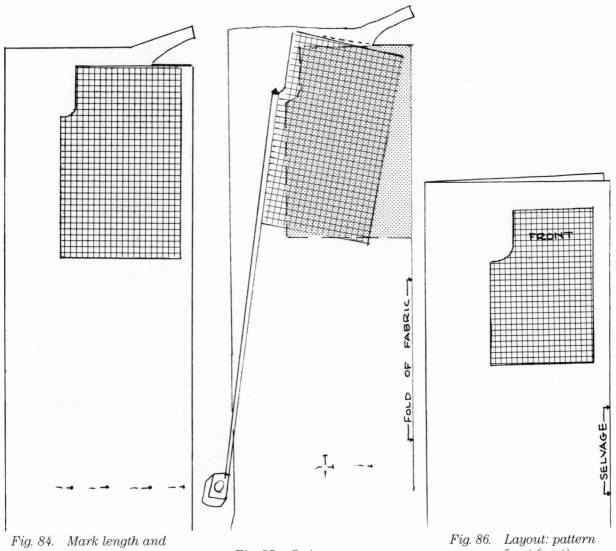

Fig. 84. Mark length and
        cut across top.

Fig. 85. Swing pattern.

Fig. 86. Layout: pattern
        front (coat).

SEWING METHOD: COAT

Sew the shoulder seams of the yoke and topstitch along the seam lines, if desired. Pin-baste the body back to the yoke, beginning at the outside edges. Ease the body fabric into the yoke, pleating the excess at the center back; then sew. Continue construction, using the commercial shirt method detailed in "Sewing Methods: Pullovers." The coat will hang nicely from the yoke and swirl gracefully at the hemline.

As for your collar, a large funnel collar, a conventional tailored type, a banded neckline, or a fur collar (from another coat or jacket) could complete this coat for an elegant effect.

For your unlined coat, all seams should be bound off neatly, because the inside of the coat will be very visible. The overlock machine is the fastest and easiest way to complete the seam edges. All seams can be trimmed and bound simultaneously. An alternative method is to use a narrow nylon-tricot strip available in precut rolls to give the inside of your coat a clean finish. This type of seam binding is available in colors and blends with the fabric for an almost invisible finish.

MORE COAT IDEAS

This design could easily be used to make a reversible coat, with wool for the outer shell, water-repellent poplin for the opposite side. Fabric combinations of this type are warm enough for spring and fall in a colder climate and comfortable all year in the more moderate areas. It could also take the place of several coats in your wardrobe. Topping the coat with a detachable hood adds style and practicality (Fig. 87).

Fig. 87. Coat with detachable hood.

JACKETS

The directions given earlier in this chapter for the coats will also serve for jacket styles. A good length will range between 27″ and 32″ for a comfortable, longer jacket and from 21″ to 24″ for the waist-length type, depending on your height (Fig. 88). For any jacket, it is wise to measure your length to assure filling your personal needs and wants.

Fig. 88. Two jacket styles.

Cut the jacket in a straight-line style directly from the pullover pattern; it can be belted later for a smart more fitted look (Fig. 89). A flared or swingback jacket would obviously look better flowing freely from the shoulder or yoke line. Made from taffeta or other stiff, dressy fabric, this feminine style could top a straight skirt or full-length pants for party wear (Fig. 90).

• Wear two unlined jackets in cooler weather: The underneath jacket can be belted or sashed (to double as a blouse); the outer one can hang loosely. Two jackets ensure added warmth.

• Try a vest *over* the jacket (instead of underneath) for a different fashion statement.

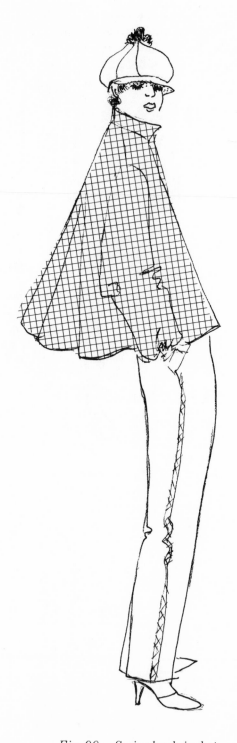

Fig. 89. Belted jacket.

Fig. 90. Swingback jacket.

64

TUNICS, VESTS, AND OTHER VARIATIONS

The title for this section needs some explanation as the words "tunic," "vest," and "tabard" are often used interchangeably in fashion references. All of these garments are most commonly found in a sleeveless form, usually worn to embellish another item of clothing. They primarily cover the torso and/or part of the upper legs (Fig. 91).

Fig. 91.   Tabard, tunic and vest.

Tunic refers mainly to the length of a loose garment, usually sleeveless, which can range from below the hips to the knee, 29″ or more. Worn by ballet dancers over a leotard, by the ancient Greeks, Romans, and Egyptians, as the principal item of clothing; in medieval times to cover a shirt and britches; by more recent generations, to disguise real or imagined figure faults.

A *vest* in European countries is an undershirt, but in the United States it is a sleeveless outer garment that is readily removable, with buttons at the front, or pulled over the head. Often worn under a jacket, over a blouse or shirt, a vest supplies a little additional warmth. The length of a vest can range from waistline to hipline and, occasionally, is seen as long as floor length.

A *tabard* is constructed from two lengths of fabric that are connected at the shoulders with an opening in the center for the head. It has some type of belt or tie closure at each side near the waistline to hold the two segments of the garment together. These open sides allow easy access to pant or skirt pockets.

Earlier in this century, a tabard was called a "sandwich board" and was used to transform a human being into a walking billboard. In its current form, a tabard can be as short as hip length or as long as the floor.

Each of these items is an important fashion statement as they add color to your wardrobe and can define your individuality with decorative treatment. A tunic, vest, or tabard made to match specific pants or skirts can be just as handsome with items of contrasting colors and harmonizing fabrics. All of these styles lend themselves to evening or at-home wear as readily as they do office attire or sportswear.

To sew any of these wardrobe extenders, use the yoke and body sections of your basic pullover pattern.

GENERAL DIRECTIONS: FRONT BUTTONED VEST AND TUNIC

Back. Begin with the back of the pattern. Place the pattern piece on the fold when using plain fabric. You have the option, at this point, of either cutting the yoke separately, or cutting the body in one piece. Again, if you use the yoke for the front of the garment, keep the continuity of the design and also use the yoke for the back. The only necessary alteration may be the length; take your measurement, compare it to the actual length of the pattern, and use your tape measure to lower the hemline, if necessary.

Front. Since this vest has a front opening, the front will be cut in two sections (as you did for the coat), either cutting the facings *with* the body sections or as separate pieces. Seam binding, foldover braid, or ribbing may be substituted for the facings around the neckline and arm openings. You can create your own bias binding from matching or contrasting fabric; or you may prefer to finish the garment with another decorative trim.

TABARD

The tabard is another vest style that is fun to wear (Fig. 92). It is cut with a one-piece front and a one-piece back, left open at the sides. The sides can be finished with tabs, decorative hooks, straps, or any other type of closure you can dream up.

Cut the tabard from the body and yoke of the pullover pattern. You can edge-line the tabard with contrasting fabric to make it reversible, or you can use conventional lining fabric. Edge-lining is exactly what its name implies: lining a garment all the way to its edges, resulting in a reversible garment. This is an easier finishing method than working with conventional facings, interfacings, etc.

To edge-line the tabard: Cut the outer shell and the lining separately from the same pattern pieces. Sew the outer shell together, front and back, at the shoulder seams. Then sew the front and back of the lining together at the shoulder seams. Place the two sections (outer shell and lining) together with the right sides facing each other. Sew completely around the outer edges of the tabard. Leave the neckline unstitched to allow you to turn the garment to the right side. To close the neckline, try either of these methods:

Fig. 92.   Tabard.

1. Fold a narrow hem to the inside to conceal the raw edges of both outer shell and lining, pin the hems together and topstitch on your sewing machine with matching or contrasting thread.

2. Fold and pin a narrow hem towards the inside of the neckline. Slip-stitch the two sections of the garment together by hand.

MORE PATTERN VARIATIONS: DRESSES

The same pattern you used for that comfortable pullover will also yield several delightful dress styles that can be worn for casual or fancy occasions by merely changing accessories (Fig. 93).

The first style is cut as a one-piece dress without a yoke (Fig. 94). Using the top pattern as it was drafted will result in a dress similar to the one in the drawing. The pullover pattern is wide

Fig. 93.   Accessorize your dress.

enough to accommodate the hips without any alterations. You can shape the dress by adding a belt.

DRESS WITHOUT YOKE

For this style, fold the fabric lengthwise to the width of the pattern back. Lay the pattern piece on the fabric fold with enough allowance at the bottom to carry the hemline to your skirt length (Fig. 95). For the straight-line dress, cut the side seams from the armhole opening to the new hemline, following the lines of the shirt pattern. Add about 3″ to 4″ to the length for generous blousing at the waistline and the hem facing.

Fig. 94.   Dress without yoke.

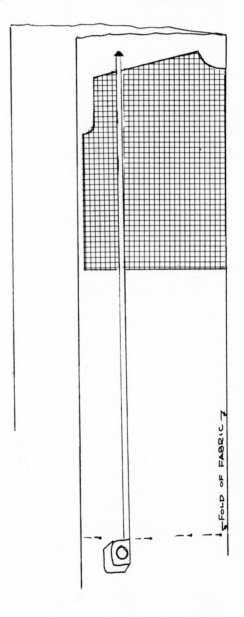

Fig. 95.   Layout: one-piece dress.

(Adding a belt will draw the dress up at least that much, so be sure the finished dress is long enough to suit your needs.) Cut the front, back, sleeves, and whatever neckline finish you've chosen. The belt, collar, and other details can come from the excess of the fabric width.

In another interpretation of this style without yoke, this dress is cut directly from the pattern across the shoulders and armholes but swung to the width of the fabric from the armscye to make a moderate A-line.

After cutting around the shoulders and armholes, extend your tape measure to the length you have chosen for this dress. Mark the new hemline on the fabric with pins or chalk. Swing the tape measure from the outer edge of the armhole to the outer edge of the hemline (the width of the fabric), and cut along the lines indicated (Fig. 96). Cut the front, back, sleeves, and choose a neckline treatment.

There is no collar suggestion for these styles because the neckline treatments from other pattern variations are adaptable for these dresses. Choose one that pleases you.

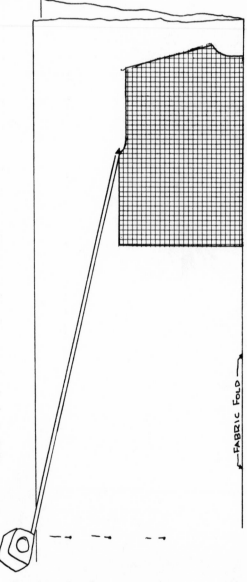

Fig. 96. Layout: one-piece dress (A-line).

SEWING METHOD: DRESSES

The construction method for these dresses is identical to that used for the original shirt.

• Sew the shoulder seams.

• Attach the collar.

• Add the sleeves.

• Sew the side seams and sleeves in one continuous line of stitching.

• Complete the casings and add either elastic or drawstrings at the ends of the sleeves.

Daytime dresses can be converted to evening wear—at-home, or evening-out clothes—by cutting them either mid-calf length or to the floor, instead of to street length. For the longer styles you will probably want slits at one or both sides of the skirt for comfortable walking (Fig. 97).

Fig. 97. Evening dresses.

DRESS WITH YOKE

If you love loose, voluminous clothes that are totally unrestricting, this is the dress for you (Fig. 98). The lightly banded neckline and gathers below the yoke allow for the easy flow of fabric. Try it in East Indian cotton for summer, corduroy or wool for winter, denim for all seasons.

Use the separate yoke pattern for this style. As you cut, shorten the depth of the neckline to 2½″ at the front and 1½″ at the back (Fig. 99). Leave the width as is. Cut the sleeves the same as the original pattern. For the collar, use a 5-inch strip that can fold over at the neckline or a 2½- to 3-inch strip that will stand up around the neck, creating a lovely frame for your smile.

Fig. 98. Dress with a yoke.

Front. Cut the yoke, adding a seam allowance at the lower edge. To cut the body of the dress: Fold the body of the pattern on the center line and place it on the fabric with the armhole near the selvage and the top of the pattern near the cut edge of the fabric, leaving a seam allowance at the top. Use the entire width of the fabric for the body of the dress. This width will be gathered into the yoke when you sew the dress together. Measure to your desired length and mark the new hemline. This dress will look better in a slightly longer length.

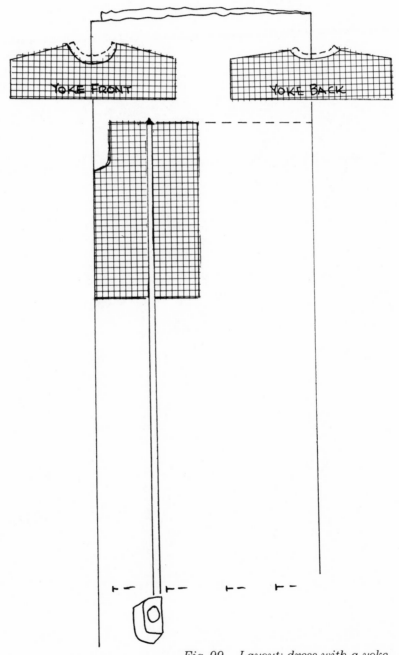

Fig. 99. Layout: dress with a yoke.

Cut the remainder of the armhole (body section) at the selvage side of the fabric. Cut straight across the upper edge of the body to the fold of the fabric. Cut straight across the hem edge.

Back. Cut the back the same as the front. To complete, gather the upper edge to fit the width of the yoke, both front and back. Pockets are added at each side; the dress can be machine hemmed.

These variations are exactly what they claim to be: ideas. Use them freely with the patterns you draft. Let them inspire your own creativity. When fleeting ideas and inspirations do come to mind, make notes and/or sketches for future reference. Your variations and original designs will be available when you need them.

Two Skirts and Assorted Variations

Ever have a day when nothing you put on felt right? You took clothes off the hangers, tried them on, and piled them on the bed (which rapidly took on the appearance of "ye olde junk shoppe" (Fig. 100). When you reached the point of despair, you ached for an old standby, a favorite

Fig. 100.   Decisions on "What to wear?"
            aren't always easy.

skirt—something in your wardrobe you could always rely on. You wanted the fit to be right, the length correct, and the waist where it should be. You looked for that feeling of total comfort.

You were searching for *the* skirt, the one you reach for when nothing else will do, the skirt that could go on any trip, whether it be an hour of shopping at the local mall or a month in Europe.

It's the perfect skirt, the problem-solver when all else fails. Well, if you are not the proud possessor of a skirt like that, the time has come to own one.

Finding one pattern to fit this description is enough of a challenge. In this chapter, you will find two patterns plus an assortment of variations.

Fig. 101.   *Sew a dirndl skirt.*   Fig. 102.   *The second design is a circle skirt.*

76

The first pattern design is a simple dirndl, a gentle A-line with adjustable fullness (Fig. 101). This basic skirt can be cut without a pattern; but since you will want to repeat the design again and again, I suggest that you make a permanent pattern or sloper for your files.

The second pattern design is a half-circle skirt with only one seam (Fig. 102). This, too, can be cut without a pattern as easily as with one. It is a style suitable for softer, more flowing fabric, a style that lends itself to graceful length variations.

Your personal pattern file is truly incomplete without these simple, basic skirt patterns (Fig. 103). Each has an absolute minimum of pattern pieces. Either skirt offers the option of drawstring or elastic waistband. Since the waistband can be cut as a foldover section at the top of the garment, there is not even a separate pattern piece to cut for the waist. Without shaping or intricate details, these are probably the easiest patterns to create, the easiest garments to sew. These skirts can be cut out and put together with lightning speed. You will fly from concept to fin-

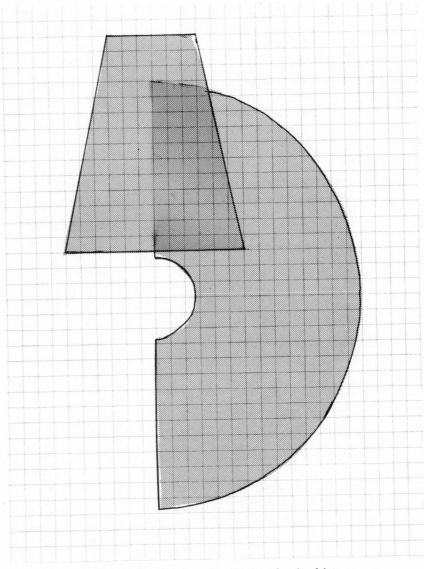

Fig. 103. Patterns for the two basic skirts.

ished garment in record-breaking time. Each skirt you sew from these personal patterns could easily become the mainstay of your wardrobe. It will fit you as no other skirt ever has.

You can draft both patterns in a comfortable street length, which can be adjusted from mini- to maxi-length with a stretch of your tape measure. Each style can be varied by choosing from some of the alternate finishing details suggested at the end of the pattern-drafting instructions.

DRAFTING THE FIRST PATTERN: DIRNDL SKIRT

For the first skirt pattern you will need two sheets of pattern paper, each approximately 30″ by 40″ or large enough to accommodate the complete front and back sections of the pattern. Always draft complete pattern pieces (both left and right halves of the front and back) whenever you create a pattern. Plaids, fabrics with repeat patterns, and suedes should never be cut from folded fabric. Cut these in single layers on the unfolded fabric to be sure that the patterns match exactly. Having complete patterns from the start eliminates the need for stopping to extend a pattern for use with specialty fabrics.

These two skirt patterns are based on the following measurements:

SIZE	HIP MEASUREMENTS
Large	38″ to 43″
Medium	35″ to 40″
Small	32″ to 36″

The measurements overlap from one size to the next. Determine whether you want your finished skirt full and flowing, or if you prefer it to hang closer to the body for a slimmer look. For the fuller look, draft the pattern in the larger size. Elastic at the waistline controls the fit.

Take two personal measurements for this pattern (Fig. 104):

1. Measure your width around the widest part of your hipline. This skirt is a pull-on, and the width at the top should be sufficient for you to step into the skirt without straining the seams or casing.

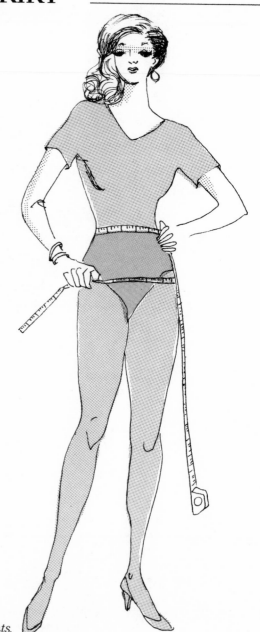

Fig. 104. Take your measurements.

78

2. Measure the length from your waist to a comfortable hemline. This measurement might vary with the style of skirt. Check your choices of length for straight skirts, A-lines, and wide hems currently in your wardrobe. These measurements should be noted on patterns of similar style for future reference. They are important to any sewing you will do. Fashions change and as time passes, these notations will tell you whether you can still use each pattern as drafted or if you will have to make adjustments before cutting the garment.

PATTERN BACK

The first chart is an overview of the pattern (Fig. 105). All measurements for the skirt pattern are noted on this illustration.

Start by drawing the center line down the

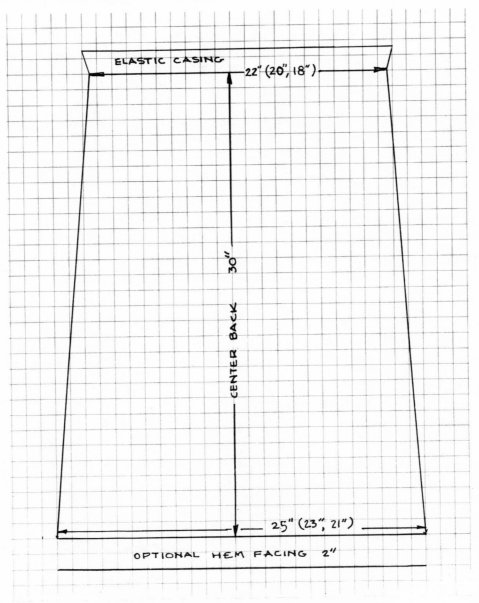

Fig. 105.   Overview of the pattern measurements.

length of the pattern paper (Fig. 106). The vertical measurements will be sketched across this line.

1. Approximately 3″ down from the top of the page, draw a dash across the center line to indicate the true waistline.

2. Draw a second slash across the pattern 2½″ above the waistline. This is the line for the attached casing. It will accommodate either a drawstring or 1″ elastic.

3. From the waistline marking, along the center back line, measure and mark the finished length you prefer for this style of street-length skirt. This is the hemfold line. Write the measurement on the center back line, if you have not already done so.

4. Add 1½″ to 2″ for a hem allowance below the hem fold. This is adequate for the most opaque fabrics. When working with soft sheers there are hem options to choose from. A narrow rolled hem is adequate but a deep hem (approximately 10″

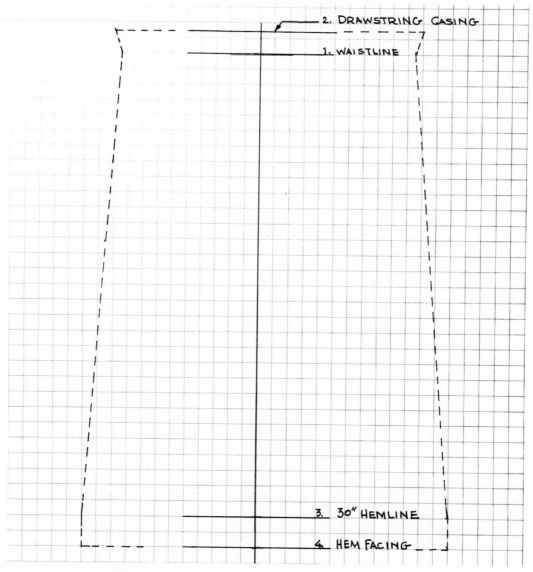

Fig. 106.   Chart for measuring the verticals.

for street length, 15″ or more for floor length) adds to the luxurious appearance of the fabric and the finished garment.

The following horizontal measurements will be drawn across the lines you have just completed. All dimensions necessary to complete the pattern are indicated on the illustration (Fig. 107).

5. Mark the waistline measurement across the top of the pattern, half the amount on each side of the center line (22″, 20″, 18″). Be sure there is enough clearance for your hips.

6. Complete the casing line across the pattern, parallel to the waistline.

7. Indicate the width at the hem edge (25″, 23″, 21″). Measure and mark off the total number of inches across the bottom of the pattern, half of the measurement on each side of the center line, where you marked the length or hem-fold line for the finished skirt.

8. Mark the hem facing across the bottom of the pattern, below the hemline.

Complete all pattern lines as follows:

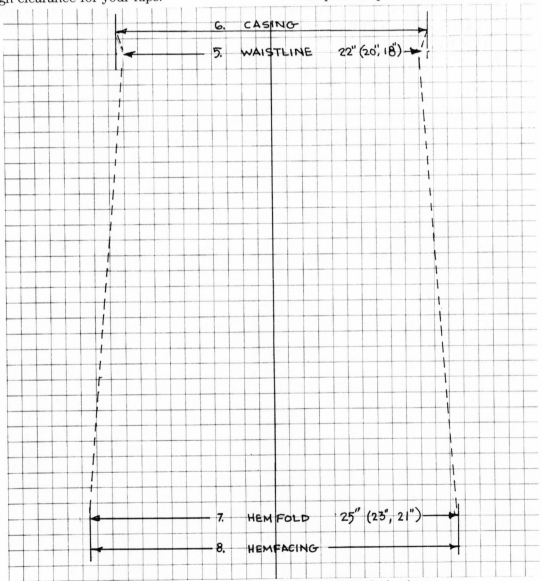

Fig. 107.   Measurements for marking the horizontal points.

• Complete the drawing of the waistline and casing line, if you haven't already done so. Mark the space above the waistline: CASING. The side seam lines will hang from the outer points of the waistline.

• Draw the lines for the hem and facing completely across the pattern between the marked points.

• Angle a line down from the outside measurement of the waistline to the outer point of the hem on each side of the skirt. These are the outside seam lines. Connect the hemline and hem allowance and you have completed the back section of the skirt pattern.

PATTERN FRONT

The back and front of this pattern are almost identical. Instead of drafting a second section for the front of the skirt pattern, trace all lines from the completed back section of the pattern *except* the waistline and upper edge of the casing. Indicate the position of these two lines with a dash across the *center front*. You will then create a slight dip at the center front to accommodate the natural curve of the waistline (Fig. 108). A ¼" to ½" slope is adequate at the center front of the pattern to prevent the skirt from buckling below the waistband.

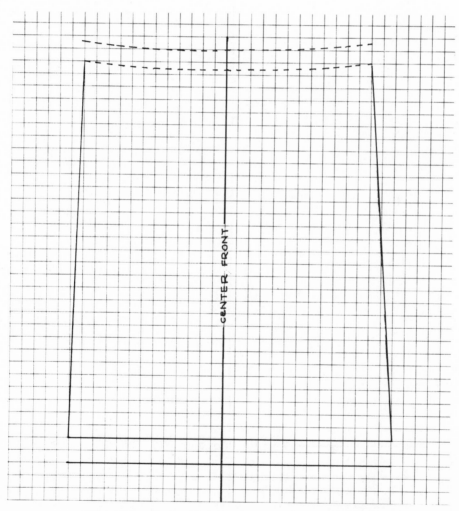

Fig. 108. Curve the front to accommodate the waistline.

Mark the center front drop and gently curve the line from the top of the side seams to the lower mark you drew at the center front. Repeat the marking below the casing and curve the line of the casing to match the line drawn for the waist. Label the pattern piece and note the size, and other details.

DRAFTING THE PATTERN FROM MEASUREMENTS

If you are larger or smaller than the average measurements given on the above skirt charts, or just want to draft your skirt pattern from more personal numbers, use the two measurements you took before the pattern-drafting instructions: the width at the widest part of your hips and your skirt length.

Start drawing the pattern as in the earlier instructions:

1. Draw a line down the center of the pattern paper to indicate the center back.

2. Measure the length of your skirt along the center back line.

3. Mark the location of the true waistline and casing lines on the pattern.

4. Take half of your hipline measurement and add 3″ (a combination of ease and the style of the skirt). The result is the measurement for the width of the waistline for the front or back pattern piece.

5. For the hemline width, take half of the hipline measurement and add 5″ for stride room and A-line shaping.

Complete all pattern lines, following the instructions previously given.

SEPARATE WAISTBAND

There may come a time when you only have a skimpy skirt length of leftover fabric that you'd really like to use. You know you can squeeze the skirt sections from the small piece you have, but there isn't enough fabric to include the drawstring casing and hem facings as part of the garment. The casing can be cut as a separate unit by using a strip of fabric along the selvage, at least the same size as your hip measurement plus 1″ for the seam allowance. To determine how wide the band should be to enclose the elastic, use twice the width of the elastic plus ½″ for a seam allowance at each side. For example, 2″ elastic will require 4½″ of fabric for the casing plus ½″ seam allowance—a total of 5″ wide. The skirt top can be gently gathered to the waistband as you sew the skirt together.

Lace seam binding (½″) or false hem facing (2″) can be stitched close to the bottom edge of the skirt for either hand or machine finishing.

BEFORE YOU CUT THE GARMENT

If you are working with a napped or directional fabric, such as velvet or corduroy, notice that this fabric will often appear to be much darker when brushed in one direction, noticeably lighter in the the other. Choose the direction of the nap that you prefer; place *all* pattern pieces in the *same* direction to ensure a total match for the entire garment.

Directional and patterned fabrics require additional yardage for matching. With repeat patterns, you might have to drop a garment section as much as one-half to three-quarters of a yard to find a pattern match. This is not lost fabric; small pattern pieces such as pockets, facings, collars, and cuffs can be cut from these large scraps. Occasionally, they will even yield a scarf or shawl.

When you are ready to purchase your fabric, take the pattern pieces to your favorite shop and lay them out on the fabric you desire. Then you'll be sure to purchase the correct yardage. Remember to note yardage requirements on the pattern for future reference.

Determine all style and finishing details before you start to cut. Changes in finishing details can also change the placement of the pattern pieces for cutting. This could affect yardage requirements. Know what you are going to do before you cut. Once you put the scissor to the fabric, it's too late to change your mind!

FINISHING DETAILS

There are many ways to complete this skirt. The following style interpretations are made from the basic pattern (Fig. 109).

1. *Wrap look* (Fig. 110): Create the look of a wrap skirt by allowing an additional 2″ at one side seam. Sew the unchanged side seam from bottom to top. Sew the augmented seam, starting from a point 10″ to 12″ above the hem fold and sew to the waist. Fold the flap that was added and topstitch to the seam line, overlapping the sections.

2. *Topstitched* (Fig. 111): Sew side seams and topstitch at one or both sides of each seam. The hem allowance can be shortened to 1″ and the entire hemline can be turned up and topstitched by machine.

Fig. 109. *Skirt variations come from the basic A-line pattern.*

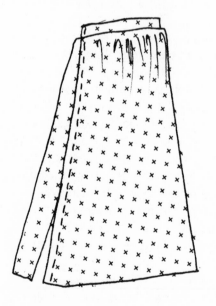

Fig. 110. *The wrap look.*

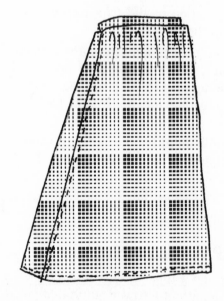

Fig. 111. *Topstitch the skirt for a more tailored styling.*

3. *Side slits* (Fig. 112): Sew the side seams, leaving a slit open at the bottom of either one or both sides.

4. *Slot seams* (Fig. 113): Sew slot seams at either side with matching or contrasting fabric for the inserts. This requires a strip of fabric the length of the skirt and at least 1″ wide. With right sides together, stitch a strip of contrasting fabric to either side of the FRONT with a ¼″ seam. Stitch the BACK along the opposite edges of the strip. Turn garment to the right side and topstitch, folding the side seams of the skirt slightly over the strip as you sew to create a small pleat over the inserted strip of fabric.

5. *Button placket* (Fig. 114): Create a placket or just the appearance of a placket for one or both sides of the skirt. Add either snaps or buttons, sewing them on through all thicknesses of the fabric. These closures can be purely decorative, as this skirt is designed to be a pull-on.

Fig. 112.   Include side slit for walking ease.

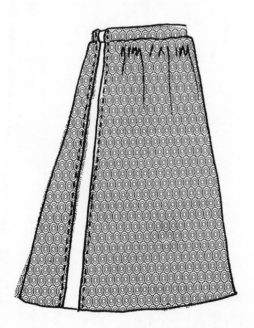

Fig. 113.   Slot seams can match or contrast with the body of the skirt.

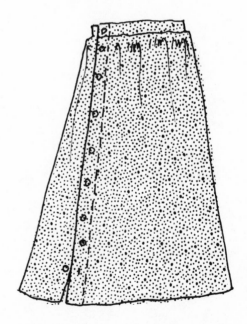

Fig. 114.   Create a button placket.

SEWING THE SKIRT

Sewing the garment from bottom to top seems to result in the smoothest finish for the side seams and the least amount of fraying at the seam edges. Stitch the skirt and finish the side seams by following any of the methods listed above. You can finish the hem by hand or machine with blind-stitching or topstitching.

Cut a piece of 1″ elastic, 2″ less than your actual waistline measurement. Form into a ring and stitch. Fold the casing extension over the elastic ring and topstitch around the top of the garment, enclosing the elastic.

This is an extremely simple skirt that will probably be sewn in less than an hour, but don't be deceived by its ease of completion. The results will be elegant and wearable.

SKIRT PATTERN VARIATIONS— EVENING LENGTH

The length of the new skirts you make from the basic pattern can be varied at the cutting board (Fig. 115). To make a mid-calf- or floor-length skirt, place the pattern directly on the fabric. Measure down from the waistline to the desired

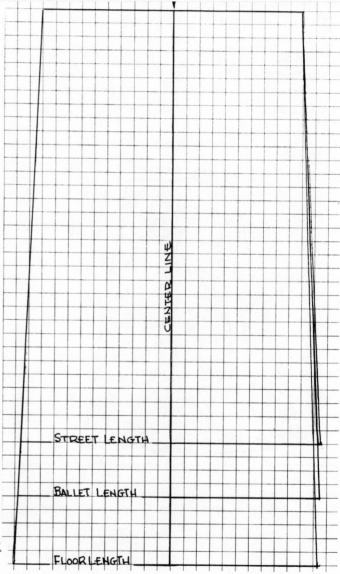

Fig. 115. Vary the length at the cutting board.

length by placing the tape measure or yardstick along the center line. Mark the location of the new hemline by inserting a pin through the fabric. Now measure the added length and indicate it across the entire width of the fabric. Continue the angle of the outside seam line to meet the new hemline of the skirt. Note this measurement directly on the pattern piece for future use. This will yield a softly flowing skirt that will hang well when made from almost any type of fabric (Fig. 116). Machine-stitch a narrow hem.

SKIRT PATTERN VARIATION— STRAIGHT SKIRT

To create a floor-length skirt that hangs straighter, lay the pattern on the wrong side of the fabric with the center back on the fold. Make sure you've left enough allowance at the top to clear the casing. Measure the extra length from

Fig. 116. An evening skirt from the original pattern.

the waistline to the point you've chosen for the longer hem. Mark that length directly on the fabric with pins, pencil, or a bit of soap. Measure the width for the bottom of the skirt (half of your hip measurement plus 4″). Roughly draw this measurement with an equal amount on each side of the center back line. Draw the new side seams by connecting the markings for the waistline to the new hemline. Complete the casing lines.

When you narrow a skirt, be sure to include slits, at one or both sides, add pleats, or insert godets to provide enough room for you to walk comfortably.

DRAFTING THE SECOND PATTERN: CIRCLE SKIRT

A piece of jersey or challis might inspire a much fuller, more flowing, skirt. If your fabric doesn't call for a design or texture match, you can take out your tape measure, tailor's chalk, or pins and forget about a pattern—just cut out a skirt directly from the fabric. If you do feel the need of a pattern, this is certainly the easiest pattern to draft (Fig. 117).

The following details will include directions for a half-circle skirt with an elastic or drawstring waistline, a full-circle skirt, and a number of waistline variations. These styles can be cut either from the general sizing provided in the table that follows, or from your own measurements and calculations. If you are extremely small or thin or have a waistline greater than 30″,

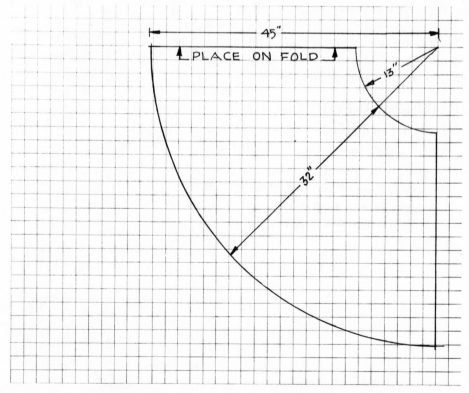

Fig. 117. Pattern for the circle skirt.

you should do your own computations for a more personal fit. The information to convert your own measurements into a pattern follows the general sizing chart. Check this table for measurements closest to your own.

☐ **Small—**
size 8 and under: 9″ (waistline formula)
☐ **Medium—**
size 10, 12:   11″ (waistline formula)
☐ **Large—**
size 14, 16:   13″ (waistline formula)
☐ **Extra large—**
size 18, 20:   15″ (waistline formula)

When you establish which waistline radius will work best for you, add approximately 32″ for the skirt length and you will have the minimum width for the fabric needed. (Example: a *medium* waistline plus the 32″ skirt length requires 43″ of fabric width.) If you wear a longer or shorter length in a full skirt, adjust accordingly.

The above measurements do work successfully and can eliminate a lot of mathematical gymnastics. But don't be deceived by the numbers. If you like a full skirt *very* full, use the figures for the larger size; if you prefer less fullness, you might even want to drop down to a smaller size.

To do your own calculations:

1. Measure your hipline and divide the measurement by 3. If you come out with fractions of an inch, round the figure off to the next highest whole number. *Example*: 9⅛″ will become 10″ for ease of handling. The resulting number is the radius for the waistline of your step-in skirt.

2. Add 1½″ to your actual skirt length for a waistband seam allowance and machine-stitched hem.

3. Proceed according to the directions for the pre-charted skirt.

Following the pattern-drafting information there will be directions for adapting the pull-on circle skirt to one with a zipper closure and interfaced waistband.

PLANNING THE CIRCLE SKIRT

The half-circle skirt is approximately 45″ from the apex of the circle to the actual cut edge of the hem. This rough figure includes the radius of your waistline (as suggested above) plus the actual skirt length. The waistline seam and hem allowances are included with these figures. Translating this into yardage requirements means that this skirt will call for approximately 2½ yards of 45″ fabric. Fold the fabric across the width, matching the selvages at each side (Fig. 118). This crosswise fold becomes the center front line of the skirt; the seam will be at the center back.

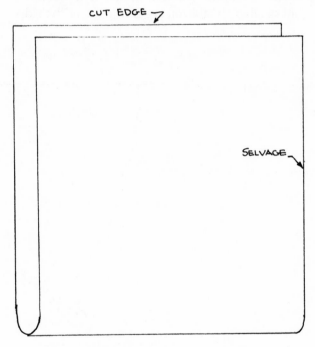

Fig. 118. Fold fabric across the width.

The length of a full skirt will probably vary from that of a straight-line skirt. To make a full skirt flow nicely, you might want an extra inch or two. Measure several full-skirted garments in your closet to be sure of the length you really want to use.

Add the skirt length you choose to the waistline radius plus ½" hem allowance (to turn up around the bottom). This total is the actual measurement that will be used to cut around the outside of the skirt.

Unfold the fabric from the lengthwise fold and refold it on the crosswise grain, selvages together. Lay it out on the floor or other large, flat surface where the fabric will not be pulled or stretched out of shape while you are trying to cut the skirt.

That would totally distort the finished garment.

To cut this skirt without first cutting a pattern, secure the end of your tape measure to the corner of your fabric (at the fold) with a pushpin, florist's pin or hatpin. Stretch the tape to the total measurement of the skirt—length plus waistline radius—to be sure the entire measurement fits on the fabric (Fig. 119).

Draw the waistline first. Move the extended tape measure around the apex in a semicircle, inserting pins or drawing short dashes with a pencil, chalk, or sliver of soap to indicate the waistline. Repeat the process to draw the line around the outside hem edge of the skirt. Cut along the lines you have indicated.

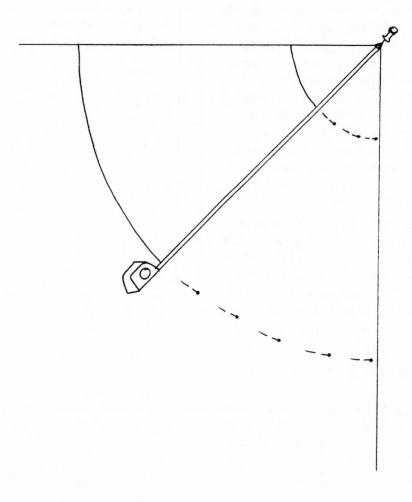

Fig. 119.   The measurements for the circle skirt.

SEWING METHODS:
SKIRTS WITH POCKETS

If you are planning to add pockets to this skirt, sew them in first, before any construction is done. A slash pocket would complement this style of skirt. When completed, this style can give the appearance of a welt pocket.

For each pocket, you will need a fabric rectangle 6″ wide by 20″ long.

1. On the outside of the garment, mark the size and angle of the pocket opening (Fig. 120).

2. With right sides together, align the short end of the pocket strip along the center line for the pocket opening and stitch (Fig. 121).

3. Bring opposite ends of the pocket strip to the center line for the pocket and sew (Fig. 122).

4. From the wrong side of the garment, open the line between the two rows of stitching, cutting tiny V's at the each end (Fig. 123).

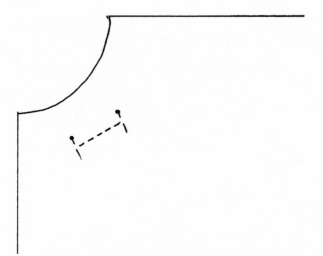

Fig. 120. *Mark the size and angle of the pocket opening.*

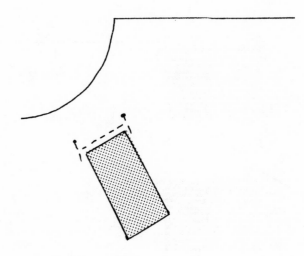

Fig. 121. *Stitch the pocket end.*

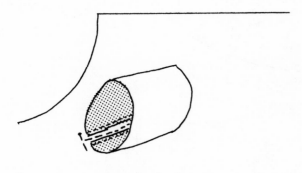

Fig. 122. *Fold and stitch the opposite end.*

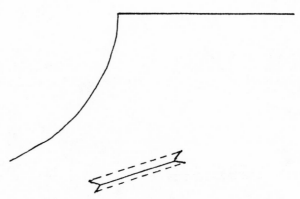

Fig. 123. *Open the line between the stitching.*

5. Pull the pocket to the inside (Fig. 124).

6. Open the V's out flat and stitch across each end (Fig. 125).

7. Turn the garment to the right side and stitch-in-the-ditch completely around the entire opening: along both ends, across the top and bottom of the pocket. Stitch carefully to avoid catching the pocket under the needle as you sew (Fig. 126).

8. Stitch down both sides of the pocket (Fig. 127). Complete the center back seam.

If the measurements you've used to cut the skirt bring you to the end of your fabric and you don't have enough room for the waistline casing, cut a separate waistband for this skirt. A strip from the selvage, 2½″ wide by the measurement of your hipline, plus 1″, will do nicely. Sew it around the raw edge at the waistline.

Cut a piece of 1″ elastic, 2″ less than your actual waist measurement. Stitch closed, forming the elastic into a ring. Turn the casing at the top of the skirt, folding the fabric over the elastic; then stitch.

Roll a ½″ hem at the bottom edge and topstitch by machine.

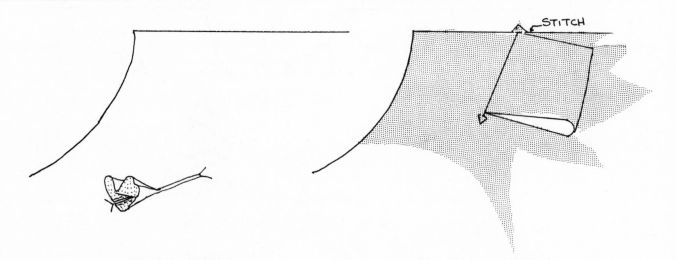

Fig. 124.   Pull pocket through the opening.

Fig. 125.   Stitch across the extensions.

Fig. 127.   Close the pocket sides.

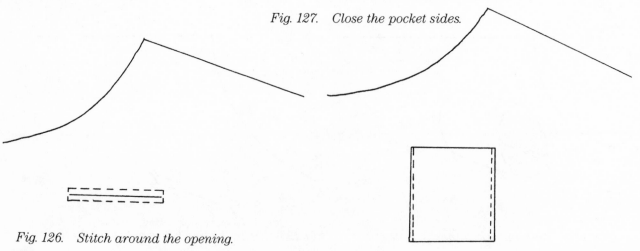

Fig. 126.   Stitch around the opening.

VARIATION—CIRCLE SKIRT

For print fabric that must be matched, maneuver the pattern before pinning to the fabric. For creating unusual pattern matches, you might even want to cut the skirt into four or more panels (Fig. 128). This will give you the opportunity to change the configuration of the fabric design.

This style of skirt lends itself well to a huge assortment of fabrics. It is elegant as a floor-length evening skirt or ballerina-length cocktail skirt. The circle skirt is extremely flattering to most figures and adapts well to unusual hemline treatments.

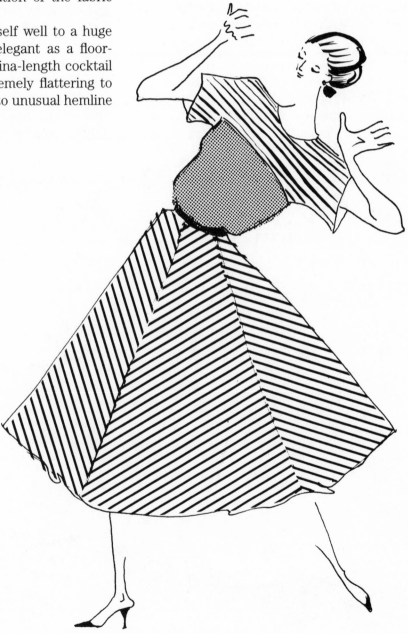

Fig. 128.   Cut the skirt in four panels for an interesting fabric variation.

• A lace strip can be stitched around the hem edge, giving a lingerie-type treatment to the finished skirt. Ruffled eyelet can also be used for a very attractive and feminine look (Fig. 129).

• Create a scalloped hem with a long zigzag or blind-hemming stitch on your sewing machine. Since machines vary so much, it would be difficult to give you an exact setting for your machine. Experiment with different lengths and widths of stitches and see what your machine will do (Fig. 130).

• Starting approximately 10″ above the bottom edge, add rows of embroidery with assorted cams and different colored thread (Fig. 131).

ADDING A ZIPPER

A zipper and interfaced waistband can be added to this skirt. Sew a 7″ or 9″ zipper into the back seam, using any method you prefer; or just follow the directions enclosed with the zipper. For heavy hips and thighs, the longer zipper is more comfortable; it allows additional room to step in and out of the garment.

Cut a waistband the size of your waist plus 3″ for the overlap and interface the band. It can be anywhere from 2″ wide to whatever height you would like to wear. High-rise waistbands have had popularity through the years and are made the same as any other waistband. They do make the waistline appear smaller (Fig. 132).

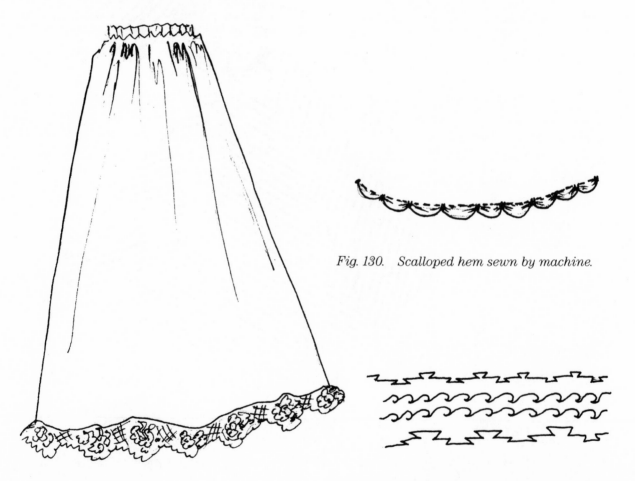

Fig. 129.   A lingerie treatment for your skirt.

Fig. 130.   Scalloped hem sewn by machine.

Fig. 131.   Combine machine embroidery stitches for an unusual hemline treatment.

Pin the waistband to the skirt at front, back, and each side, overlapping the ends, 2″ at the front, 1″ at the back (Fig. 133). Gather or pleat the excess fabric of the skirt to fit evenly around the band; then stitch.

You can also create a sashed waistband: Cut a strip of fabric approximately 12″ wide by 60″ long. This is attached to the waistline of the skirt by centering the sash at the front and just stitching

Fig. 133.   Pin the waistband to the skirt.

Fig. 132.   A high-rise waistband is very flattering.

around the waistband. Leave a gap at the back to allow access to the skirt and room to tie the bow. Fold the piece in half lengthwise and stitch-in-the-ditch, completing the finished sash. There are any number of ways to wear this sashed waistband. Wrap the sash around the waist; cross it in back and tie it in front or at the side (Fig. 134). Wear this one high and scrunched. Tie the sash at the back and secure it with a big bow for a flirty, little girl look (Fig. 135).

Fig. 135.   Tie a back-wrapped sash into a big bow.

Fig. 134.   Tie a sash at the side.

VARIATION—BALLERINA SKIRT

The ballerina skirt is another variation of the circle skirt that is fun to wear. It is an extremely full, shinbone-length skirt that is made by cutting two half-circles for the skirt, instead of one (Fig. 136). This style requires two complete fabric lengths or approximately 5 yards. The inseam pockets are sections cut from the scraps and sewn with the side seams. Cut a separate waistband that is large enough to pull over your hips. This skirt can be made with either elastic or a drawstring at the waistline, making a zipper unnecessary. Be sure you use firm elastic for the waist. The extra panel will make the skirt a little heavier than previous styles, and you don't want to keep pulling at it to keep it in place. Two or more of the remaining triangles left after cutting this circle skirt can be sewn together, forming a large shawl.

Add a drawstring over an elastic ring to provide a little more security. Insert drawstring eyelets at the center front of the waistband before you turn the casing and enclose the elastic ring. Thread the drawstring through the same casing.

You can gather or pleat this skirt to an interfaced waistband. Insert a zipper at one side. A narrow hem can be sewn by machine.

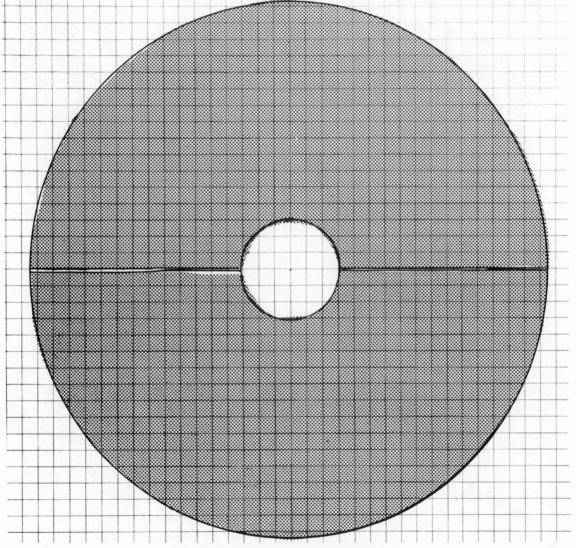

Fig. 136.   Pattern for a ballerina skirt.

Full skirts really need fluffy petticoats (Fig. 137). A petticoat or two will provide the support a full skirt needs to drape gracefully. (See the chapter on Accessories for details on making your own petticoats.)

VARIATION—WRAP SKIRT

The basic circle skirt pattern will also yield an elegant wrap skirt. Make it of corduroy, tweed, brocade, or silk, for anything from casual to dressy wear. Street length or floor length, wherever you hang your hemline, a wrap skirt can be counted on to add a touch of glamour (Fig. 138).

Cut the CIRCLE SKIRT pattern as it was drawn, but cut a separate waistband from the selvage of the fabric.

The skirt will hang better if one open end is faced. Add a 12-inch-wide strip of fabric to the

Fig. 137.   Full skirts need fluffy petticoats.   *Fig. 138.   Count on a wrap skirt for elegance.*

edge that will overlap. Lightly interface or include ½" twill tape with the seam, as you sew. This will give the outer panel a little more body. The opposite edge need only be folded under 1" and stitched (Fig. 139).

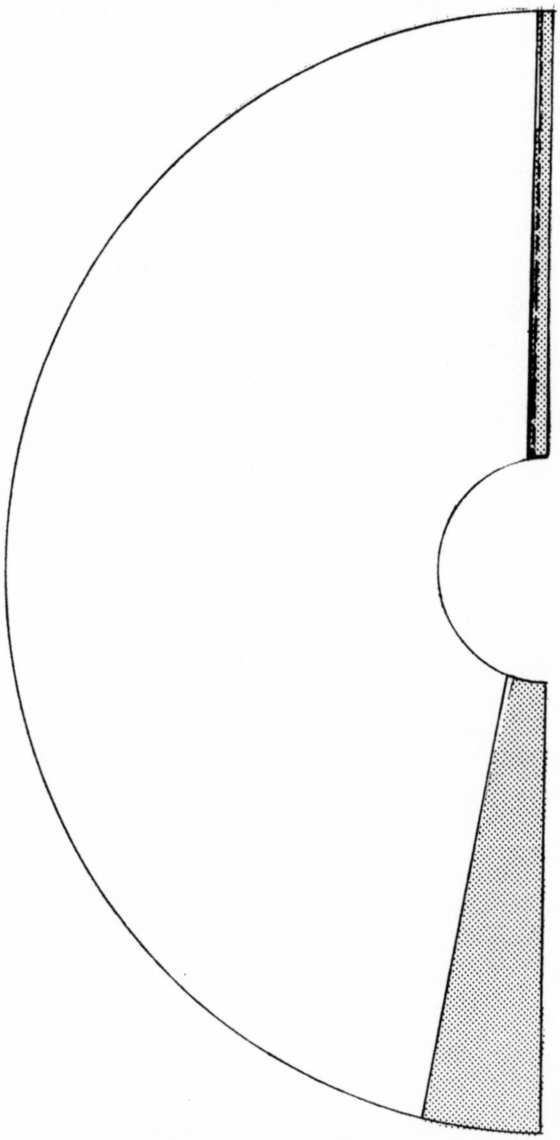

A wrap skirt can be bound all the way around with foldover braid. The bottom corners of the overlapping sides can be slightly rounded for ease of handling. Ease the braid gently around these curved corners to prevent it from drawing up after it is stitched. For square corners, mitre the braid. The same braid can either be added to the waistband or used instead of the matching fabric band to keep the continuity of the skirt. Decorative ribbon, sequinned edging, or soutache braid will also give this skirt a fancy finishing touch.

There are two ways to complete a waistband for a wrap skirt.

1. Cut a waistband to the size of your waistline plus 2" to 3" extra to accommodate the overlapping ends. The waistband can be secured with buttons, snaps, or grip fasteners (Fig. 140).

2. The second band is 2½" wide by twice the measurement of your waistline plus enough length to tie into a bow. Attach the band around the entire waistline to overlap with the skirt when it is wrapped around you (Fig. 141). Tie the ends in a knot or a bow.

Fig. 139. Diagram for making a wrap skirt from the circle skirt pattern.

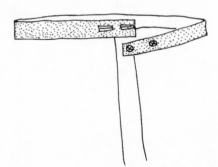

Fig. 140. Sew a buttoned waistband.

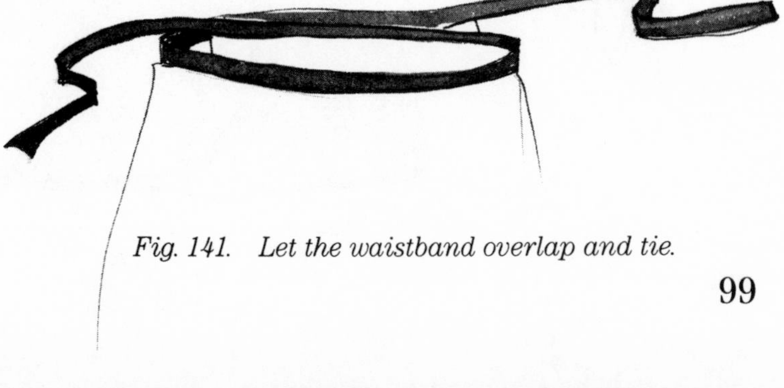

Fig. 141. Let the waistband overlap and tie.

Either of these skirts can be closed at the front or back (Fig. 142).

Wrap skirts can also work into longer lengths quite successfully. Just follow the directions for adjusting the length of circle skirts. Wear any of these wrap skirts with patterned hose that match your blouse or sweater. It's a fun way of dressing.

Wrap skirts, or any skirt for that matter, can be backed, lined, or worn with a separate slip.

• To back a garment: sew the lining and outer fabrics together as a single layer.

• To line a skirt: Complete the lining and outer layer separately. Then sew the two sections into the waistband. Each "skirt" is then hemmed.

• A separate half-slip is often referred to as a liner. It is a valuable accessory that can be worn under any unlined skirt or dress in your wardrobe to prevent fabric sag.

Fig. 142.   You can wrap this skirt to the front or to the back.

MORE VARIATIONS—DRESSES

Either of these patterns can successfully be combined with the pullover pattern in the preceding chapter for an additional dress style.

• Use each pattern without making any changes or alterations. Cut the basic top but omit the collarband. You are creating a crew neckline in the new version (Fig. 143). Sew bias binding, seam tape, or lace seam binding around the crew neckline. Turn the tape to the inside; then topstitch. Cut the dirndl skirt and sew the top and skirt together, overlapping the waistlines to form an elastic casing. Use either ¾″ or 1″ elastic at the waist. Fold up a ½″ hem and topstitch by machine.

• Finish the neckline with a simple, rolled edge. Cut a separate cowl that will add versatility to the neckline (Fig. 144). This could be a strip of fabric, either bias cut or straight, 10″ to 20″ deep by enough width to go over your head easily when stitched. Sew the single seam and finish the hems by machine.

• Cut the top with a 2½″ to 4″ allowance below the true waistline for blousing; this time, include

Fig. 144.   *Sew a separate cowl for your dress or blouse.*

Fig. 143.   *Make a dress from the skirt and pullover patterns.*

101

the stand-up collar. Use the circle skirt pattern for the bottom half of the dress (Fig. 145). Ease the skirt and top together. This style can be worn either belted or loose. If the waistlines of the skirt and top are overlapped 1¼″ and stitched, you again have a built-in elastic casing.

These suggested styles could work for anything from street length to floor length, from sheer linen to sweat-shirt fabrics.

Sweatshirt or fleece fabrics have become a very popular and practical fashion statement.

Fig. 145.   Another style of dress using the top with the circle skirt.

These clothes can be popped into the washer and dryer and put right back on again. They need no ironing and can be rolled up in a backpack or duffle bag when travelling. Garments from this fabric have been seen at the opera, office, and shopping mall. When you sew them yourself, you create a fashionable and inexpensive wardrobe of coordinated separates (Fig. 146). Try using huge shoulder pads for a very exaggerated look, or no padding for a more natural appearance. However you plan your sweatshirt separates, the fun of them is in the exciting array of colors and the total comfort they afford. If you tire of these fashions for daily wear, use them for beach cover-ups and exercise clothing instead of plain old sweats. The glamour can go on and on.

Fig. 146.   Fleece or sweatshirt fabric separates.

Pants

Early in the 1980s, a few leading lights of the fashion industry tried to convince women that pants would no longer be a valid fashion statement. They were soundly hissed and booed by a large portion of the buying public and laughed at by most home sewers. Pants have become too much a part of a woman's world to be given up by anything short of major warfare or an act of Congress.

But, while most women find pants to be the ultimate answer to their wardrobe needs, there are those with figure problems that defy trouser comfort in any form. Pants must be comfortable to totally integrate a wardrobe: They should be long enough at the rise and rounded through the crotch to follow the shape of the body. The crotch bed (the base curve of the crotch between the front and back rises) should not bind, ride up, or hang halfway to the knees. The available fabric for sitting should be ample. In other words, the pants should *fit* (Fig. 147).

Designed to fulfill all of the above requirements, these drawstring pants are very complimentary to round hips and thighs. The design is soft and easy (not figure-hugging and revealing) and also flatters the less-than-round figure by suggesting curves where they don't exist. These loose pull-ons hang approximately an inch above the ankle—a comfortable, cropped length. Drawstrings at the waist and ankles control the width of the pants as well as the length. These pants can be worn in many ways. Allow them to hang loosely around the ankles, and they have the flow

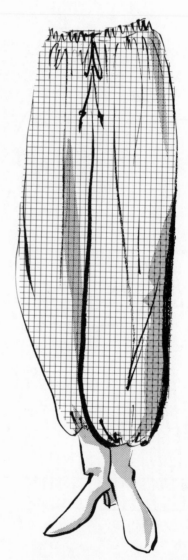

Fig. 147. Drawstring pants designed to fit.

104

of full pants while remaining totally under control (Fig. 148). Tighten the strings to fit the ankles and they will hold the bottom of the pants to your boots (Fig. 149). Pull them up to the knees for the look and length of knickers (Fig. 150). Wrap a long sash around your waist, allowing it to drape over your hips for a narrower, more controlled, look (Fig. 151).

These pants team well with the pullover pattern in this book and any of the styles created from it. Match the pants and top for a jumpsuit look while still maintaining the convenience and versatility of two pieces (Fig. 152); or create a jumpsuit for one-piece comfort. Make a matching jacket and/or coat for an elegant pants suit (Fig. 153). Set off the pants with a contrasting top. For example, twill pants can be topped with a medium or lightweight fabric of strong color. A strong color on top will balance the weight of a heavier, gathered fabric used for the pants.

The style of these pants adapts well to all types of fabrics. Select corduroy, gabardine, canvas, or flannel of natural or blended fibres for all seasons except summer. Lightweight cotton, sheer wool, or linen are the best fabric choices in warmer weather. Silks in any form—knitted or woven—are always elegant and luxurious. This pattern can be used with knitted fabric, such as cotton interlock, wool, or blends of double knits, and varieties of sweater knits.

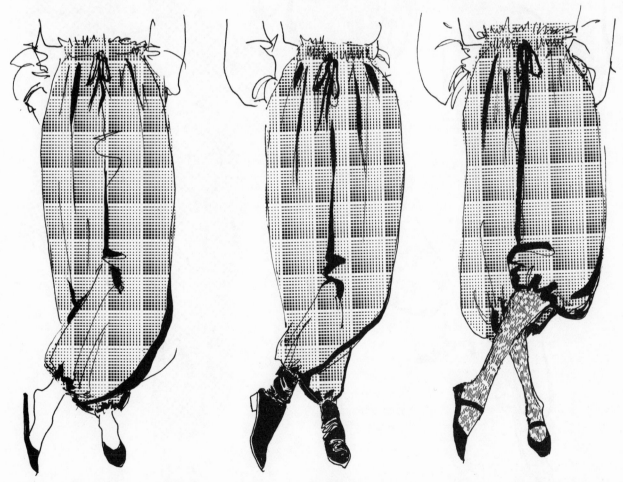

Fig. 148.   Drawstring pants worn loose and flowing.

Fig. 149.   Drawstring pants with a tucked-in look.

Fig. 150.   Drawstring pants like knickers.

Fig. 153. With matching jacket or coat, the result is an elegant pants suit.

Fig. 152. Drawstring pants worn with a matching top.

Fig. 151. Drawstring pants sashed at the hips.

DRAFTING THE PATTERN

Before you draft your pants pattern, verify your personal measurements (Fig. 154). Drafting the pattern in the wrong length will not give the results you want. If your legs are very short or very long, the measurements given for the pattern will not apply to you. These will have to be adjusted before you begin drafting the pattern. Drop a tape measure from the waistline to the floor while wearing low-heeled shoes. Make a note of that measurement, including the height of your heels. That total is usually equal to the actual length of the pants including the hem facing.

You will need two sheets of pattern-drafting paper, approximately 30″ by 45″. Collect your pen or pencil and a yardstick. A dressmaker's curve would be helpful, but it isn't absolutely necessary. Spread the sheets of pattern paper on your cutting table or the floor, allowing plenty of room to work.

Draft the front and back pattern pieces. Then you can pin or baste the pieces together and try on the pattern to fit it before cutting into expensive fabric. Trying on a pants pattern is very important. It's impossible for a single pattern that has been computed by averaging the sizes of many figures to truly fit everyone. There are too many places where individual figures vary. Personal alterations almost always have to be made.

Fig. 154.   Measure your length from waist to ankle.

A pattern that is sized from your personal measurements and requirements makes extensive adjustments unnecessary. You are creating a sloper (a permanent, personal pattern) that fits you properly and can be used for future pants designs.

Start by drafting the pattern front (Fig. 155). Follow the charts and these step-by-step directions where all measurements are repeated (Fig. 156).

FRONT

1. Draw a line, approximately 42″ long, on the middle of the pattern paper; mark it CENTER FRONT.

2. Indicate the lower edge of the casing near the bottom of the pattern paper.

3. The hem fold is 1½″ above the casing line. Add this line at the bottom of the pattern.

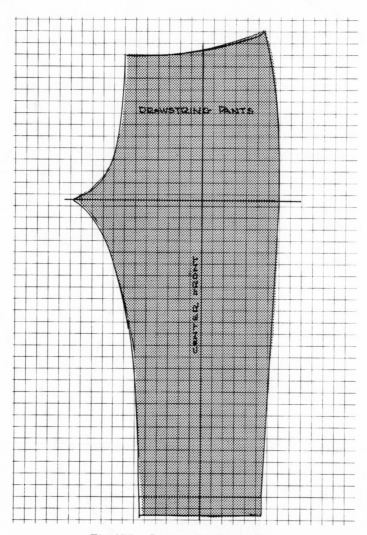

Fig. 155.   Pattern for front of pants.

4. Stretch your tape measure to the length of the pants leg: 25¾″ (25¼″, 24¾″). Mark that point and draw a line across the page to indicate the depth of the crotch.

5. There are three measurements that start from a line across the crotch that define the curve of the waistline.

• Measure the midpoint of the waistline, 13″ (12¾″, 12½″) up from the crotch line. Draw a slash across the center front line at that point.

• To the left (towards the inseam), measure and mark off 12¼″ (12″, 11¾″) for the height of the rise.

• On the right of the center line (towards the outside seam edge), mark a point 13¾″ (13½″, 13¼″) for the top of the seam.

6. Indicate the height of the drawstring casing by adding marks 1½″ above the dashes you've drawn for the waistline.

Wait until you've completed the horizontal measurements for the width of the pants before connecting the dots. The horizontal measurements are all calculated from the center front line.

The outside seam line is a straight line, angling out slightly from the waistline to the crotch and

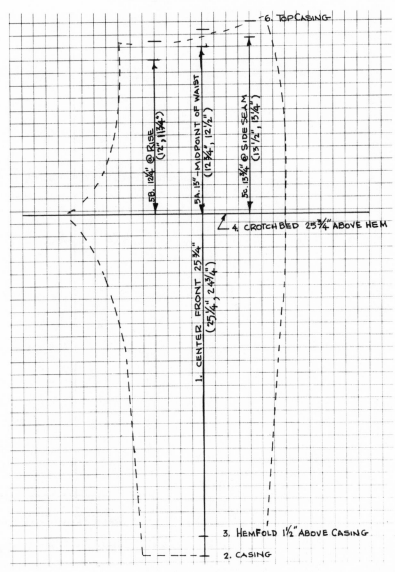

Fig. 156.   Measurements for vertical points of the front.

coming back in from the crotch to the bottom of the leg, connecting the waistline and the hem. The crotch rise will also be measured from the center line to ensure the correct width and curve for the crotch (Fig. 157).

7. Measure and draw the 11″ (10½″, 10″) width of the hem evenly across the center front line at the bottom of the leg. Draw both hem and casing lines across the pattern.

8. The width for the crotch line is 18½″ (18″, 17½″). Measure off 7″ (6¾″, 6½″) to the right of the center front and 11½″ (11¼″, 11″) to the left or inseam side. Mark these points along the line drawn for the crotch.

9. To connect the points you've indicated (Fig. 158): Place a yardstick between the outer points of the hem and the crotch line and draw the outer seam line of the leg. Connect the ends of the casing.

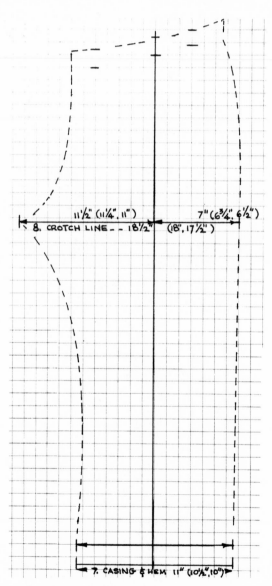

Fig. 157. Measurements for horizontal points of the front.

110

10. A dressmaker's curve can be used for drawing the curve of the inseam. Keep the first 3″ at the bottom of the inseam line straight, parallel to the center line; then curve the seam up and out to meet the outer point of the crotch.

11. To complete the upper or body portion of the pattern: The outer edge of the waistline begins at a point directly above the outer edge of the leg hem, 5½″ (5¼″, 5″) to the right of the center front line. The waistline is 12¾″ (12¼″, 11¾″) wide. Curve the line for the waist between the marks at the top of the pants. Complete the casing above the waistline.

12. The rise or center front seam of the pants is the last line that remains to be drawn between the waistline and point where the inseam and crotch bed meet. To get the correct curve for this seam: Mark off 2¼″ from the outer edge of the crotch bed. Measure up the same distance and curve the line between these two points. Angle the yardstick between the end of the curve and the waistline and complete the line. All measured points on your pattern should now be connected.

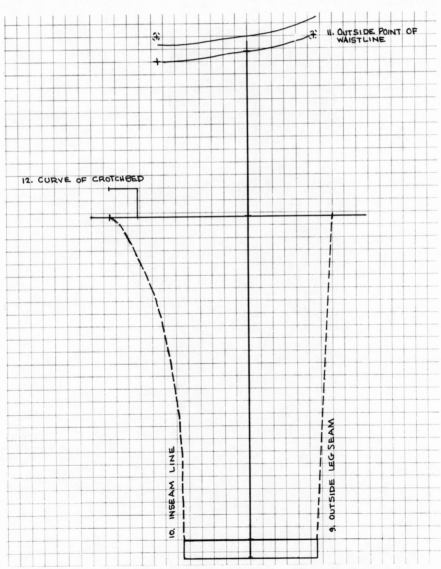

Fig. 158. Connect the marked points to complete the pattern.

Always double-check the finished pattern pieces to be sure all lines are where they belong and the proper measurements have been used. The shaping for these pants is not as critical as most trouser patterns, but you still want everything to be right.

BACK

Lay out the second sheet of pattern paper that you prepared. The method for drafting the pattern BACK (Fig. 159) is the same as for the FRONT. The measurements are detailed on the illustration for the BACK pattern.

1. Start with the vertical measurements (Fig. 160): Draw the center back line approximately 43″ long down the middle of the page.

2. Indicate the casing and the hemline at the bottom of the pattern.

3. Measure and mark the crotch bed, 25¾″ (25¼″, 24¾″) above the hemline.

You need the following three measurements to mark the curve of the waistline:

4. Mark the height of the side seam at 13¾″ (13½″, 13¼″) above the crotch seam. This matches the side seam line for the front of the pants.

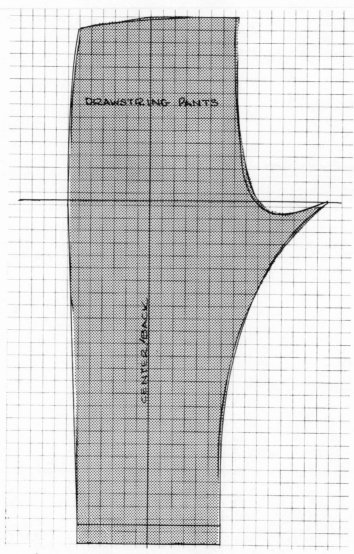

Fig. 159.   Pattern for back of pants.

5. Measure and mark a point at the top of the center back line 14½″ (14¼″, 14″) above the crotch line.

6. Mark the height of the center back rise 15″ (14¾″, 14½″) above the crotch.

7. Sketch the casing 1½″ above the waistline measurements indicated.

The horizontal measurements for the back are as follows (Fig. 161):

8. The width of the leg at the hemline and casing is 12″ (11½″, 11″). Draw this evenly across the center back line, 6″ (5¾″, 5½″) on each side.

9. The crotch line measures 21½″ (21″, 20½″). Indicate 7″ (6¾″, 6½″) to the left of the center line at the outside seam line, and 14½″ (14¼″, 14″) to the right or crotch seam side. Draw the line across the pattern.

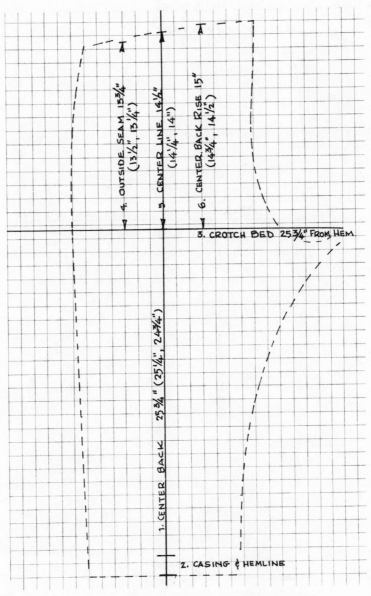

Fig. 160.   Vertical measurements for the back of the pant pattern.

113

10. The width of the back waistline is approximately 13″. To complete the waistline, start the drawing from a point directly above the outside edge of the pants hemline.

Double-check and complete all the lines for the back of the pattern. Curve the inseam and crotch rise as indicated on the chart. Be sure to label each pattern piece: FRONT; BACK.

You are now ready to try on your new pants pattern. Pin or baste the sections together and determine if the fit is correct. Check the positioning of the lower curve of the crotch bed. It should fit snugly to the body but not bind. The side seams should hang straight, forming a line that points from under your ear to your anklebone. The inseam should not pull towards the back or front but hang in a straight line down the leg.

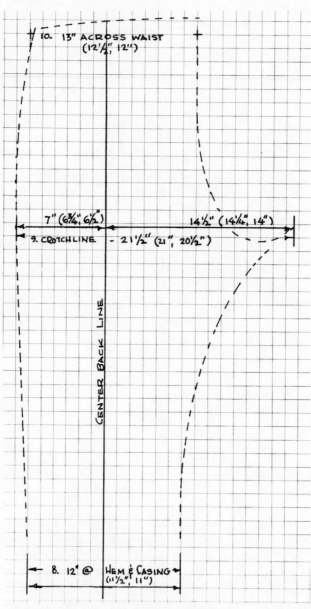

Fig. 161. *Horizontal measurements for the back of the pant pattern.*

Sit down while trying on the pattern. If the center back pulls down, this is an indication that the back rise is too short. Add ¼″ to ½″ along the top of the pattern, starting at the center back and tapering the addition to meet the topmost point of the outside seam. Make any necessary adjustments before using the pattern.

To cut these pants properly, place the center front and center back lines on the vertical grain of the fabric (parallel to the selvage). After cutting the fronts and backs, mark them with a note on a piece of masking tape to be sure the sections are sewn together properly: front to front, back to back (Fig. 162).

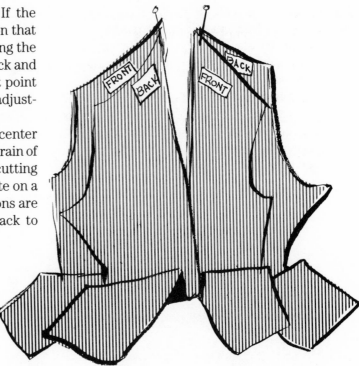

Fig. 162.   Mark pant sections to ensure sewing garment together properly.

CONSTRUCTION

Pockets are best added to the front and/or back sections of a garment *before* you begin the construction; there will be less fabric to handle. (For inseam pockets, see Index.)

Patch pockets can be added to the front or back of these pants. When you use lightweight fabrics, the pocket will retain its shape better if it is interfaced and/or lined. Self-lining usually creates the nicest finish for a pocket, but any lining fabric will serve.

Fully lined pockets are not complicated, using this method. A nice size pocket for this style of pants is approximately 6″ by 7″ (Fig. 163). For ease of sewing, you can round the bottom corners. Cut the pocket shape twice; then sew the two sections together with right sides facing each other. Stitch around the outside of the pocket, leaving a small opening at the bottom for turning

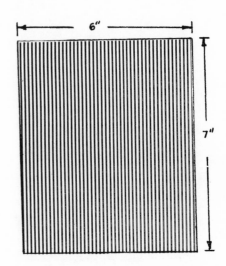

Fig. 163.   Patch pocket pattern for lightweight fabric.

it to the right side (Fig. 164). Pin the completed pocket to the garment in several places (to be sure it doesn't slip while you're sewing). Top-stitch in place, backtacking at the beginning and end of the stitching line.

Heavyweight or very firm fabrics need only a 2" or 3" foldover flap at the top to keep the pocket from sagging. For a 6" by 7" pocket, cut the shape 6" wide by 10" high (Fig. 165). The flap can be interfaced for that *quality* look; or include twill

tape along the fold line of the pocket flap to keep the pocket from rolling. Sew a narrow hem at the top of the flap. Fold the flap over the pocket with right sides together (Fig. 166). Stitch around three sides. Turn and press the facing to the wrong side of the pocket.

Sew pockets to each front section of the pants at a convenient height. Bartack or backtack at the beginning and end of the seam to secure the top edges (Fig. 167).

Fig. 164.   *Stitch around the pocket, leaving a small opening at the bottom.*

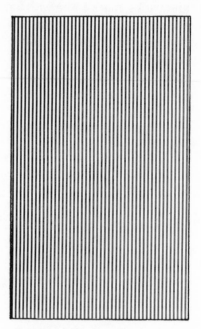

Fig. 165.   *Pattern for patch pockets, using heavy-weight or firm fabric.*

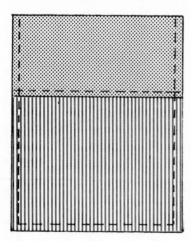

Fig. 166.   *Fold the flap over the right side of the pocket and sew.*

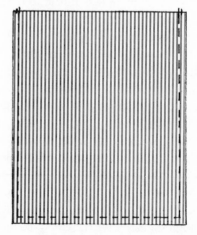

Fig. 167.   *Sew pockets to the pant sections.*

116

Pants construction methods are pretty standard but there might be something in the following two methods to make your sewing easier. If one or both of these basic methods is completely new to you, give it a try. Either one might prove to be the system you've been looking for.

The first method of pants construction is the one to use when you're sure there is no reason for any alterations, no lines are critical and the pants are loosely fitted. These drawstring pants fall into that category.

CONSTRUCTION PANTS METHOD: 1

1. Sew the outside seam of one leg, front to back, stitching from bottom to top (Fig. 168). Complete the inseam.

2. Sew both seams of the opposite leg.

3. Turn one pant leg inside out and place the opposite leg inside, aligning the crotch bed and outside seam lines (Fig. 169).

4. Sew around the crotch rise from back to front.

Even though the pattern fits you perfectly, some changes occur when cutting a garment from different fabrics. Before sewing the drawstring casing, refit the depth of the crotch to your body. Make any adjustments at the waistline. When the fitting lines are critical, try the next system.

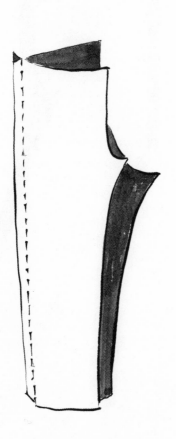

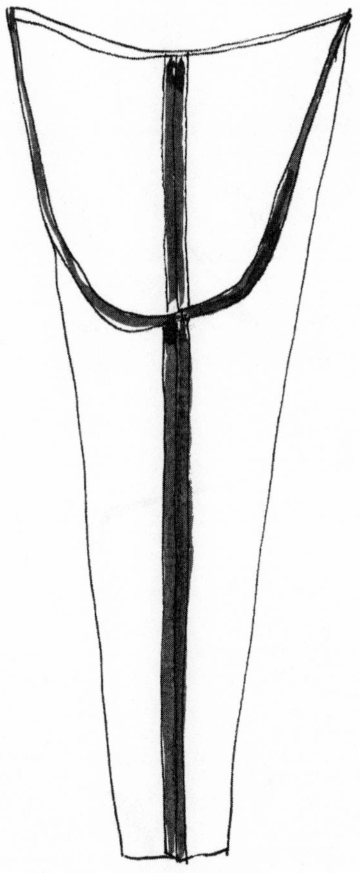

Fig. 169.   Fit one finished leg inside the other to sew the crotch.

Fig. 168.   Sew the outside seam of each pant leg.

CONSTRUCTION PANTS METHOD: 2

1. Sew the two fronts and two back sections together along the crotch rise seams (Fig. 170).

2. Complete the inseam of each pant leg by sewing the seam up one leg, across the crotch seam, and down the other side in one continuous line of stitching (Fig. 171).

3. Before you go any further, pin the side seams together and try the pants on (Fig. 172). Any necessary adjustments can be made at this point by moving the pins.

4. Then stitch the outside seams together along the pinned lines. The pants are now ready for waistband and hemming.

5. Turn the casings at the waistline and leg bottoms and stitch.

Fig. 170. Sew fronts and backs along the crotch seams.

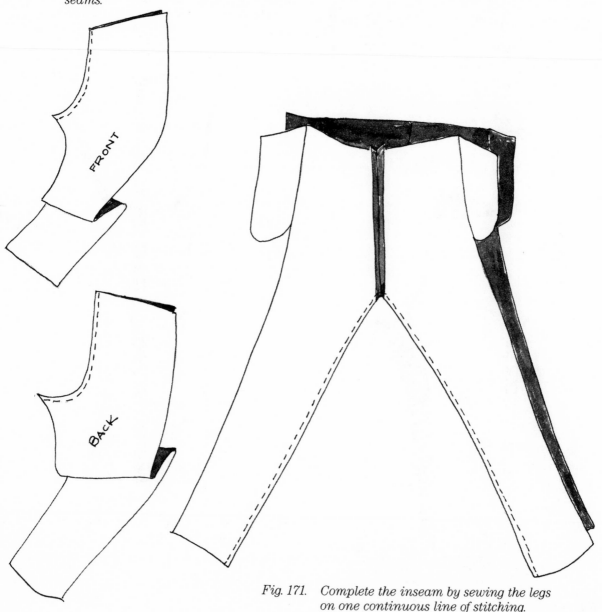

Fig. 171. Complete the inseam by sewing the legs on one continuous line of stitching.

For the drawstrings (waist and leg bottoms) you can use white, colored, or print shoelaces. They are available in a complete assortment of colors, patterns, and lengths. If you prefer to make matching drawstrings, add approximately 6″ of ¼″ elastic at the middle of the waistline string. This will allow the drawstring to breathe with you.

Fig. 172. Pin the side seams and try on the pants.

PLACKETS AND INTERFACED WAISTBANDS

The drawstring casing at the waist can easily be traded for an interfaced waistband. When completed with either buttons or a zipper inserted at the front, side, or back, the style will look totally new (Fig. 173).

To make a separate waistband, cut a strip of fabric (the size of your waistline plus 3″) from the selvage. Interface the band with sew-in or iron-on interfacing.

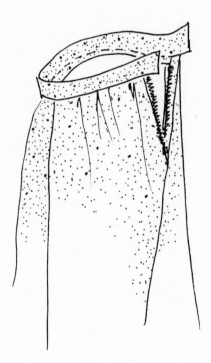

Fig. 174. Attach the waistband without interfacing.

Fig. 173. A change of finishing details creates a new style.

120

ELASTIC-LINED WAISTBAND WITH CLOSURE

An alternate method to complete the waistband: Use elastic instead of interfacing. Line the entire band with elastic to ease the gathers over the entire waistline. The elastic prevents gathers from bunching up at the back or sides of the pants or skirt. This is a particularly good system for figures with large hips and small waists; the waistband hugs close to the body but allows you to slide the pleats or gathers to the most flattering position.

1. Cut a strip of elastic the size of your waist measurement.

2. Attach the waistband to the pants top after you insert the zipper. Do not interface (Fig. 174).

3. Pin the elastic to both ends of the waistband. Without stretching the elastic, insert additional pins 3″ from each end. Fold the elastic in half and pin that point to the center back. Fold each half to find the middle of each side section and pin those points above the side seams (Fig. 175).

4. Fold the waistband over the elastic and sew, keeping the first and last 3″ even and stretching the rest between the pins to fit the fabric (Fig. 176). As you sew, do not catch the elastic in the stitching or you will lose the advantage of having the elastic free to move the gathers around the waistband wherever you want the fullness.

5. Sew buttons and buttonholes through the completed ends. The elastic provides a firm foundation for your closures.

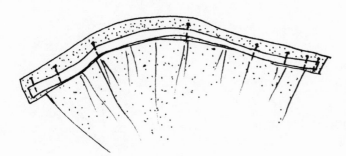

Fig. 175. *Pin elastic to the waistband above the seamline.*

CLOSURE WITH ZIPPER

1. Insert a 7″ or 9″ zipper at the front, back, or side. (For large hips, the better zipper length is 9″. It allows easier access when stepping into a skirt or pair of pants.) These pants are full enough to create a fly for the zipper without the addition of any fabric. For a back zipper, use the slot, or centered, method of installation. This covers the zipper with two equal folds of fabric. A front zipper should definitely have a fly closure, but the side zipper insertion style is optional.

2. When you have stitched the zipper, pin the waistband to the top of the garment with the ends overlapped at the opening. The overlap varies at each end: The underneath portion (or button side) extends 1″ beyond the zipper; the top end (for the buttonholes) extends 2″ beyond the end of the zipper (Fig. 177). Pin these ends in place.

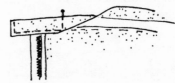

Fig. 176. *Sew the band without catching the elastic.*

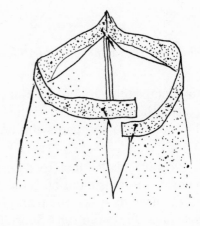

Fig. 177. *Overlap the ends of the waistband.*

Fold the waistband in half to find the center back. Pin this point to the top of the center back seam. Fold in half at each side and pin the waistband at each side seam (Fig. 178).

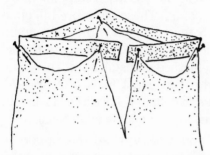

Fig. 178. *Pin waistband to the pants at front, back, and each side.*

3. Evenly pleat the top of the pants to fit the waistband (Fig. 179). Concentrate the pleats more towards the center front and back of the pants. Unpressed pleats at the sides will add bulk around the hipline. To create stitched-down pleats for these pants, pin and stitch them before pinning on the waistband. Stitch each pleat approximately 2″ to 3″ from the waistline edge. When the pleats are sewn, pin the waistband to the pants top.

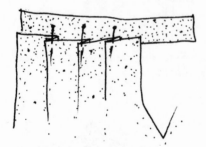

Fig. 179. *Pleat the extra fabric to fit the waistband.*

4. Stitch completely around the waistband, attaching it to the pants. Then fold the waistband over the raw edge of the pants and topstitch to secure.

5. Sew the buttonholes first to determine the placement of the waistband buttons. Attaching buttons by machine eases the pain of finishing your garments. To sew buttons: Shorten the machine stitch length to zero; then adjust the zigzag

width to the spread of the holes in the buttons. Place a pin under the button before stitching to keep the thread shank from getting too tight and pulling the buttonholes. Stitch back and forth about eight times to secure the button.

BUTTON FLY CLOSURES

A button fly can be cut separately instead of being cut as part of the garment. Determine whether you want the buttons and buttonholes to be visible and decorative (Fig. 180) or concealed under a flap.

Fig. 180. *Fly-front pants with decorative button closure.*

EXPOSED SEPARATE BUTTON FLY

1. Cut 3 pieces of fabric 2½″ by 8″ (Fig. 181).

2. Interface and sew two of these rectangles together along one long side with right sides facing each other. Create an angle (approximately 1¾″) at the bottom of the outside edge, as shown. Turn to the right side (Fig. 182).

3. For the buttonholes, start at a point approximately 2″ above the bottom edge and ½″ in from the outside edge. Sew 3 horizontal buttonholes through the flap, 2″ apart (Fig. 183).

4. Sew flap to left-hand edge of front opening, matching top edges of placket and pants (Fig. 184).

5. Open flap out, away from body of pants. Topstitch along seam line (Fig. 185).

Fig. 181. *Pattern for cutting separate fly.*

Fig. 182. *Interface the flap and sew the two sections together.*

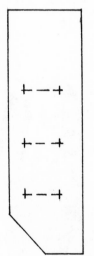

Fig. 183. *Sew buttonholes before attaching the flap to the body of the pants.*

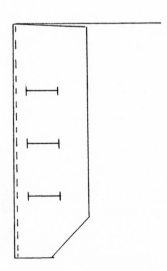

Fig. 184. *Sew the flap to the pants.*

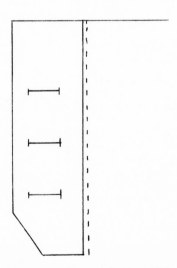

Fig. 185. *Topstitch parallel to the seamline.*

123

6. Interface the third rectangle. Hem one long side and create an angle at the bottom corner, as you did in step 2 (Fig. 182). Sew the raw edge of the opposite side to the opening, right sides together with the top of flap and body of pants matching (Fig. 186).

7. Turn facing underneath and pin to the pants (Fig. 187).

8. Sew the crotch seam. Pin bottom of buttonhole flap over the button side. Topstitch as shown, matching the tops of the fly and the buttonhole flap seam with the outside edge of the underneath section (Fig. 188).

9. Pleat the top of the pants to fit the waistband and complete the pants, as previously explained in "Closure with Zipper," steps 3 to 5. Align buttonholes of the waistband to the location of the fly buttonholes.

10. Sew on the three buttons of the fly and the two waistband buttons either by machine or hand (Fig. 189).

Try this separate fly system, using leather or synthetic suede for the fly and the waistband. It's especially elegant for a pair of wool or corduroy pants.

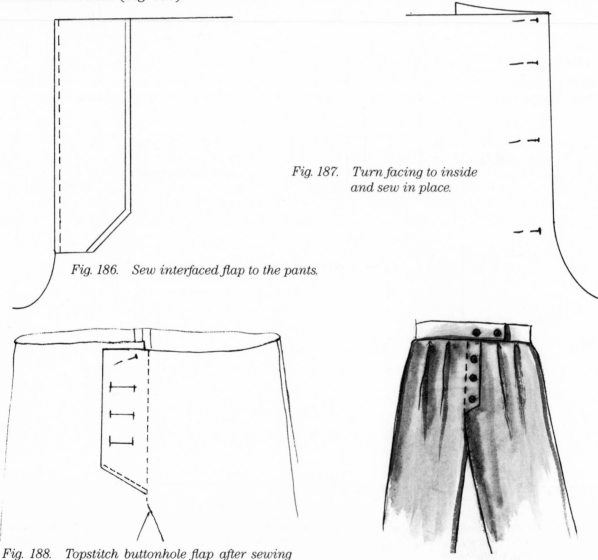

Fig. 186. Sew interfaced flap to the pants.

Fig. 187. Turn facing to inside and sew in place.

Fig. 188. Topstitch buttonhole flap after sewing the crotch seam.

Fig. 189. Sew buttons by hand or machine.

CONCEALED BUTTON FLY

1. Cut five strips of fabric, each 3″ by 8½″ (Fig. 190). One of these strips will be interfaced to serve as the facing for the button side of the opening. (The other four will be used for the buttonhole tab and concealing flap.)

2. Interface two strips and sew together along one long side. Turn to right side and make three evenly spaced buttonholes, 2″ apart, starting 2″ above the bottom edge (Fig. 191).

3. Interface and sew the remaining two strips together along one long edge and turn to right side (Fig. 192).

4. Pin flaps to pants by the following method, as shown in Fig. 193: Pin the section containing the buttonholes to the underside of the pants, with the unsewn edge parallel to the crotch rise and even with the top edge of the pants. Pin the other flap to the pants top, matching the buttonhole portion (with the pants section sandwiched between the two flaps of the fly). The bottom edges of both flaps are swung out with the lower curve of crotch crossing through the flaps, ½″ outside the bottom buttonhole.

5. Sew the flaps to the pants along the raw edges, curving the seam below the last buttonhole to match the crotch curve (Fig. 194). Trim away the excess fabric. Fold the flaps out, into position, and press. When attaching the waistband, catch the upper edges of the fly in the stitching line with the upper edge of the pants.

6. Attach the facing to the opposite side. Add the buttons by sewing through the pants and facing.

7. Sew a small triangle at the bottom of the fly to hold the flaps together and to prevent the seam from opening, as shown in Fig. 193.

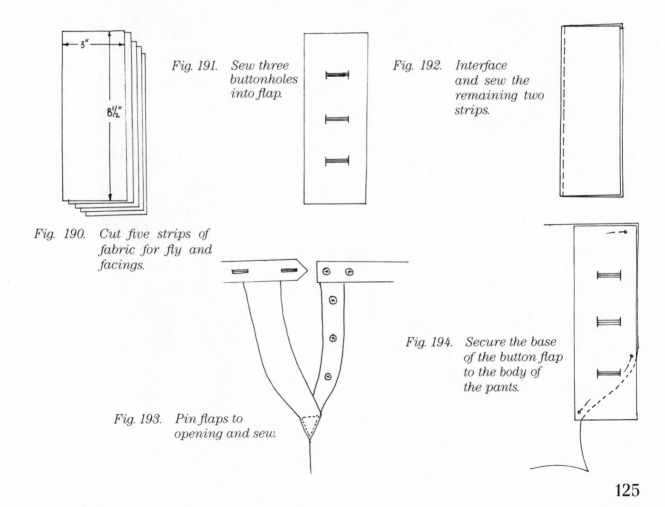

Fig. 191. Sew three buttonholes into flap.

Fig. 192. Interface and sew the remaining two strips.

Fig. 190. Cut five strips of fabric for fly and facings.

Fig. 193. Pin flaps to opening and sew.

Fig. 194. Secure the base of the button flap to the body of the pants.

ADDITIONAL STYLE VARIATIONS

• The pant legs can be changed by tapering the seams to the hem while still retaining fullness at the top (Fig. 195). The top of the pants can be trimmed to the measurement of the hips plus 2″ for ease. Taper the legs to the ankles from the widest part of the hips for a slim look. With this fitted style, there is no need to add drawstrings or elastic bands at the ankles. You can even add an elastic stirrup at the bottom. Just be sure you don't slim the pants too much or your feet won't fit through the legs! Wear these pants with a loose or smock sweater for a very slender appearance.

• Pleat each leg opening to fit the ankle, and you create a simple variation that requires no cutting changes (Fig. 196). Use the drawstring casing as a hem facing for the pants. Fold 1″ pleats around the bottom of each leg. To secure the pleating, run a line of machine stitching over the pleats, approximately 1″ above the hemline stitching. As an alternative, you may stitch down each pleat individually by machine. Try the pants on before the final stitching to be sure you haven't narrowed the opening too much to admit your foot.

• Belt the bottom of each pant leg and eliminate the drawstring casing (Fig. 197). Two D-rings placed at one end of the band will allow you to adjust the width and amount of gathering for each leg. Tack the band at the inseam on each leg to keep the bands from getting lost.

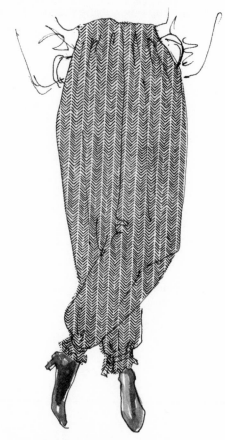

Fig. 196. Pleat around the ankles instead of using elastic in a casing.

Fig. 197. Belt the bottom of each leg.

Fig. 195. Taper the legs and finish with elastic stirrups.

126

• Make culottes from the pattern by widening the bottom of each leg. Cut straight down along the outside seam line from the widest part of the hip to the hem. On the inseam side, cut straight down from the crotch bed to the hemline without shaping the leg. After sewing the pants, fold up a narrow hem at the bottom and machine-stitch.

This style has the look of a skirt and all the comfort of well-fitting pants (Fig. 198). Make these sweeping culottes in any length and from any type of fabric you like. This style can set a definite mood for all occasions (Fig. 199).

Fig. 198. Palazzo pants are very comfortable.

127

Fig. 199.   Culottes can be cut to any length.

• Gurkha shorts are another pants variation from your original pattern. These pleated, full-legged, Bermuda-length shorts can be worn cuffed or rolled up from the hemline. They are assembled with a wide, wrapped waistband—very flattering to most figures (Fig. 200).

1. Measure your length from waistline to just below the kneecap. This is the entire length of the shorts, including the cuff.

2. Insert a zipper, creating a fly at the center front.

3. Cut a waistband the measurement of your waistline plus 6″ and from 3″ to 5″ wide. Interface the waistband. Attach it to the pants top, leaving a 1″ tab at the underneath side and a 5″ overlap on the top or buttonhole side.

4. Pleat the end of the waistband on the buttonhole side only (Fig. 201). Make the buttonholes; then sew on the buttons. Keep the high-rise waistband in place by adding a snap inside where the waistband overlaps.

Make these pants in velveteen for evening, gabardine for general wear, and lightweight fabrics for summer.

Fig. 200.   Make Gurkha shorts in a variety of fabric.

Fig. 201.   Pleat the end of the waistband.

Accessories

Sewing separates is fun, but there is more to a wardrobe than skirts, pants, jackets, and dresses. There are *slips* (to make a skirt hang smoothly) and *dickeys* (to fill in the neckline of a blouse or sweater and change its appearance). There are *scarves* and *belts* (to add a splash of color to an outfit) and *shawls* (to protect your shoulders from cool breezes) (Fig. 202). All of the above—and more—can be made with some simple directions, a swish of your scissors, an application of your overlock or regular sewing machine, some patience, and a little imagination.

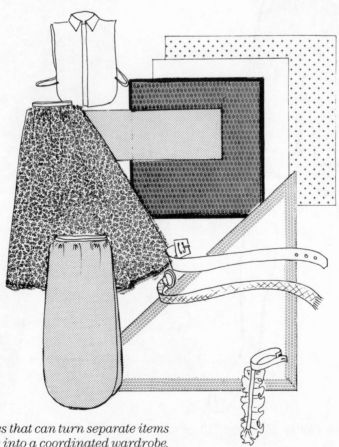

Fig. 202.   Accessories that can turn separate items of clothing into a coordinated wardrobe.

DICKEYS

Dickeys, those practical little wardrobe extenders, were once available in every department store and boutique. They came in an assortment of colors and fabrics. Today, for some strange reason, they are rarely available in retail shops.

A dickey is a little bib or blouse front that can be worn with a blouse, sweater, jacket, or dress to change its appearance (Fig. 203). A dickey can fill in or complete the original neckline of a garment when worn underneath it, or totally change the appearance of the same garment when worn over the front.

The term "dickey" originally referred to the starched shirt front worn by men for formal occasions (Fig. 204). It was a formal or dress shirt collar with only the front part of the shirt attached. Worn with a tie, a dickey took on the appearance of a complete shirt under a buttoned dinner jacket or tailcoat. It was sometimes worn over a plain, old-fashioned collarless shirt to avoid the necessity and expense of laundering a pleated or ruffled dress shirt after each wearing. Waiters freely adopted this accessory as an economy measure.

At various times in fashion history, this little item has played an extensive role in wardrobe expansion. In this century, the versatile dickey was adapted to the needs of women. A high-necked dickey was worn over a gown with a deep décolletage to turn it into a modest daytime dress; under a jacket, the dickey created the look of a blouse without the bulk of a full shirt underneath. The dickey can still serve these purposes today.

You probably have a potential dickey already hanging in your closet. An outdated shirt or knit blouse can easily be salvaged and converted into a colorful, practical dickey. You can even use a man's discarded shirt.

Fig. 203.   Make dickeys in an assortment of colors and styles.

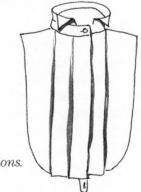

Fig. 204.   A man's dickey for formal occasions.

CREATING A DICKEY
FROM A SHIRT

Rescue that shirt from wherever it's been stored and lay it out on the cutting table (Fig. 205). Patterns won't be necessary for this quick trick, as each shirt suggests its own finished size and shape. As long as the collar and fronts of the shirt are in good condition, you only really need to eliminate the unnecessary portions.

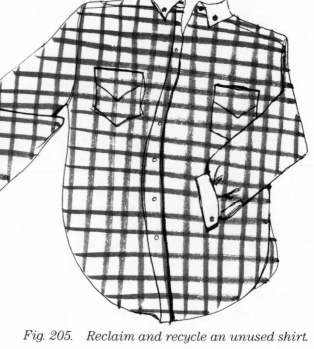

Fig. 205.   Reclaim and recycle an unused shirt.

Use a pencil or fabric pen to sketch the cutting lines directly on the shirt. Start at the front of the shirt and draw a little line half way between the fourth and fifth buttons. This seems to be a good length for almost all figure types. (The exception is a particularly bosomy woman who will need a little extra length at the front for a comfortable fit. Start the cutting line below the fifth button.) Mark the identical spot on the button and buttonhole sides of the shirt to be sure that both fronts will be of equal length.

Curve the line up about 2″ while sketching towards the side seam, creating a nicely rounded front and corner (Fig. 206). (Square corners could poke out under a sweater and form strange lumps.) Continue marking straight up along the side seam, outside the pocket (if there is one) to the shoulder. Save the pocket where it exists, particularly if using a man's shirt. The ample size gives you a protected storage area for money or keys.

Fig. 206.   Sketch the cutting line directly on the shirt front.

Mark the line over the shoulder and down the back, curving it around the bottom and up the other side (Fig. 207). Match the cutting lines at the shoulders and side edges.

If you are planning to sew this dickey on a regular sewing machine, cut it out first and overcast around the entire edge with a zigzag stitch.

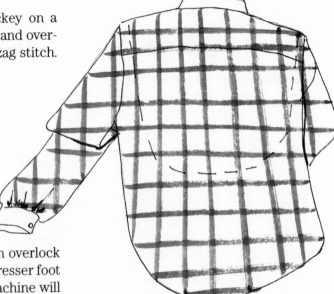

Fig. 207. Continue the cutting line around the back.

If you are finishing this dickey on an overlock machine, just put the shirt under the presser foot at the right front edge and sew. The machine will automatically cut and finish the garment for you.

The only thing that remains to be completed is the connector for the sides. If you tie the front and back together, the dickey will stay in place without twisting or riding up. The ties can be made of elastic or fabric.

Elastic Ties.   Cut two strips of ¼″ or ½″ elastic, 4″ to 6″ long. Sew one strip at each side, front and back (Fig. 208). Try on the completed dickey to be sure the elastic is comfortable. Lengthen or shorten the elastic strips for your personal requirements.

Fabric Ties.   The sides of the dickey can also be secured with ties made from scraps of matching fabric. Cut four strips of fabric 1″ to 1½″ wide and 10″ long. You can either fold each strip in half lengthwise, turn in the raw edges, and topstitch the strips, or sew a length of fabric tubing as you would for spaghetti straps. Attach at each side and tie in a flat bow.

Note your personal requirements plus any deviations from the original instructions or measurements to be sure that you have the information at your fingertips the next time you want to make a dickey.

Fig. 208. Completed dickey with elastic ties at each side.

133

CREATING A DICKEY PATTERN

A dickey pattern can be derived from the body, facings, and collar portions of almost any blouse or shirt pattern (Fig. 209). Lay out the top pattern you've chosen and prepare two pieces of pattern drafting cloth, each approximately 14″ by 18″.

The finished dimensions of the dickey will be approximately 12″ wide and 16″ long. If you are long or short waisted, be sure to adjust the length before you begin. Your dickey should not overlap the waistband of your skirt. For a large bosom, widen the pattern to 14″ or whatever amount is necessary to comfortably cover the bustline. (A narrow dickey will pull towards the middle of the body.)

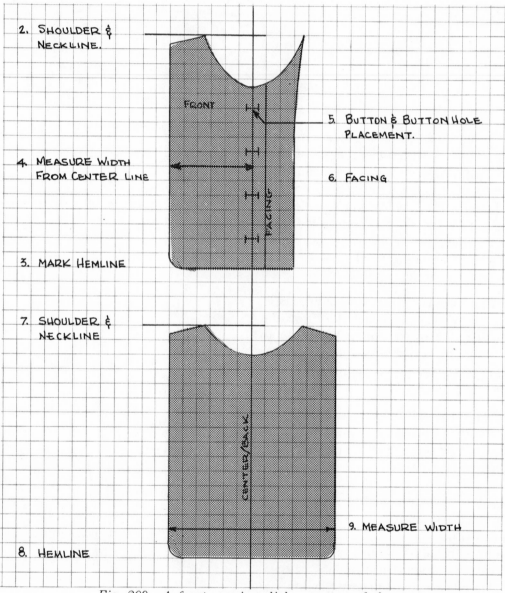

2. SHOULDER & NECKLINE.

FRONT

5. BUTTON & BUTTONHOLE PLACEMENT.

4. MEASURE WIDTH FROM CENTER LINE

6. FACING

FACING

3. MARK HEMLINE

7. SHOULDER & NECKLINE

CENTER/BACK

9. MEASURE WIDTH

8. HEMLINE

Fig. 209. A front-opening dickey pattern fashioned from sections of a garment pattern showing front and back sections.

FRONT AND BACK PATTERNS

1. Start with the front pattern section. Draw the center front line down the length of the pattern paper. Match this center front line of the new pattern to the center front line of the original pattern.

2. Trace the neckline and shoulder slope exactly as they appear on the original pattern.

3. Measure down 16″ from the point where the neck and shoulder lines meet. This is the bottom edge or hemline.

4. Measure 6″ across the pattern, starting from the center front line for the width of the dickey. (A front-opening pattern piece is cut in two sections.)

5. Indicate the placement for buttons and buttonholes.

6. Include the facing with the front of the shirt.

Place the straight edge of this pattern piece against the center/front line of the shirt and copy it creating a one piece front. (Mark this section FRONT, CUT 2.)

7. Continue with the back pattern section. On the second sheet of pattern drafting paper draw the center line and match it to the center back line of the pattern. Copy the shoulder lines and the neck opening.

8. Measure the length for the pattern and mark it on the drawing.

9. Mark the 12″ width for this pattern section, 6″ on either side of the center line.

Complete the outside lines for the pattern. Trace the collar and neckband (if there is one) at the side of the dickey pattern or on a separate piece of paper.

TURTLENECK DICKEY

A pattern for the turtleneck dickey can be drafted on two sheets of pattern paper, each 14″ wide by 18″ long. This pattern is designed for use with knits or stretch fabrics.

PATTERN: FRONT AND BACK

1. Start with the pattern front (Fig. 210). Draw the center front line down the middle of the paper.

2. Along the center front line draw a dash near the top to indicate the place where the shoulder and neckline meet.

3. Draw another dash across the center line ½″ below the peak of the neckline to designate the shoulder slope.

4. Indicate the depth of the neckline opening 2½″ below the peak of the shoulder-neckline point.

5. Measure down 16″ from the topmost point for the bottom or hem edge.

6. The width of the neck opening is 5″. Indicate the opening by drawing half this amount on either side of the center line.

7. Mark the width of the dickey: 12″ or 6″ on each side of the center line.

Complete the lines of the pattern front. Draw the shoulder lines, side edges, and hem rounding the two bottom corners. Sketch the neckline.

8. Continue with the back (Fig. 210). Draw the center back line down the length of the paper.

9. Indicate the shoulder peak and the ½″ drop for the outer edges of the shoulder lines.

10. The back neck opening is the same width as the front: 5″. The depth of the back-neckline drop is 1¾″ below the peak of the shoulder.

11. Mark the slit for the center back opening. This line extends approximately 6″ down from the point of the shoulder peak. (The slit is 4″ below the lowest point of the neckline, long enough for easy access when pulling the dickey over your head.)

12. Allow 16″ for the back length.

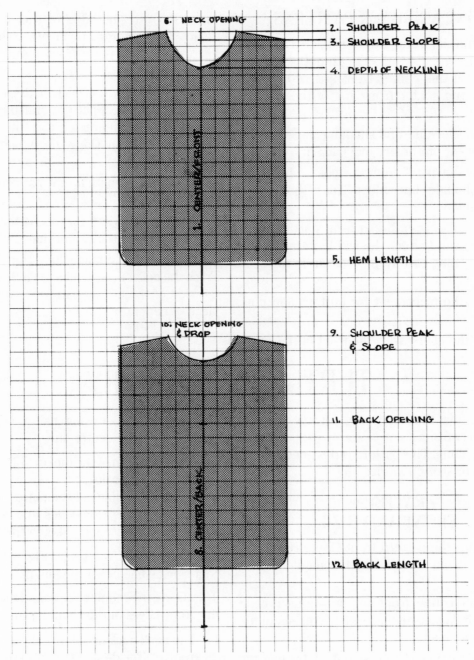

Fig. 210. Draft the front and back for a turtleneck dickey pattern.

Connect all lines for the back as you did for the front. Draw the shoulder lines and complete the neckline and opening. Round the lower corners as you draw the outside edges.

The collar is a straight strip of fabric, 16½″ long by 1½″ wide. It can either be cut on the straight grain of the fabric or on the bias. Note these dimensions on either the front or back section of the pattern. A separate pattern piece is not necessary.

CONSTRUCTION DETAILS:
TURTLENECK DICKEY

1. Sew the shoulder seams (Fig. 211).

2. Roll the hem along the slit at the back and stitch.

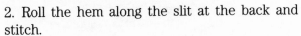

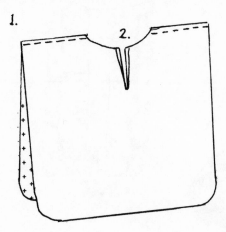

Fig. 211. *Sew shoulder seams and roll edge of back opening.*

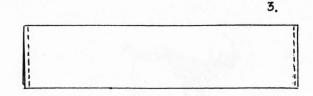

Fig. 212. *Fold collar and stitch ends.*

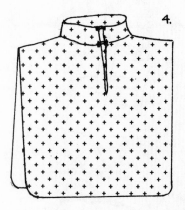

Fig. 213. *Add hooks or snaps to make the collar stand up.*

3. Fold the collar in half along the length and stitch the ends. Stitch to the dickey along the neckline. The 6½″ width folds down to a simple 3″ turtleneck collar (Fig. 212).

4. Sew either tiny snaps or hook and eye at the back opening. To make the collar stand higher and closer to the nape of the neck, add a snap at the fold line of the collar (Fig. 213).

A collar strip 22½″ by 12″ or 14″ makes an ample cowl collar. Cut the neckline ½″ deeper all the way around. Sew the cowl with enough room to comfortably admit your head without any back opening.

TRANSFORMATION DICKEY

A transformation dickey is another style that you might enjoy wearing. It is a little neckband with or without a collar, plus a fancy extension that can attach over the front of a shirt or dress (Fig. 214).

Follow the directions and check the illustration (Fig. 215). The transformation dickey is made from straight pieces of fabric and really won't need a pattern.

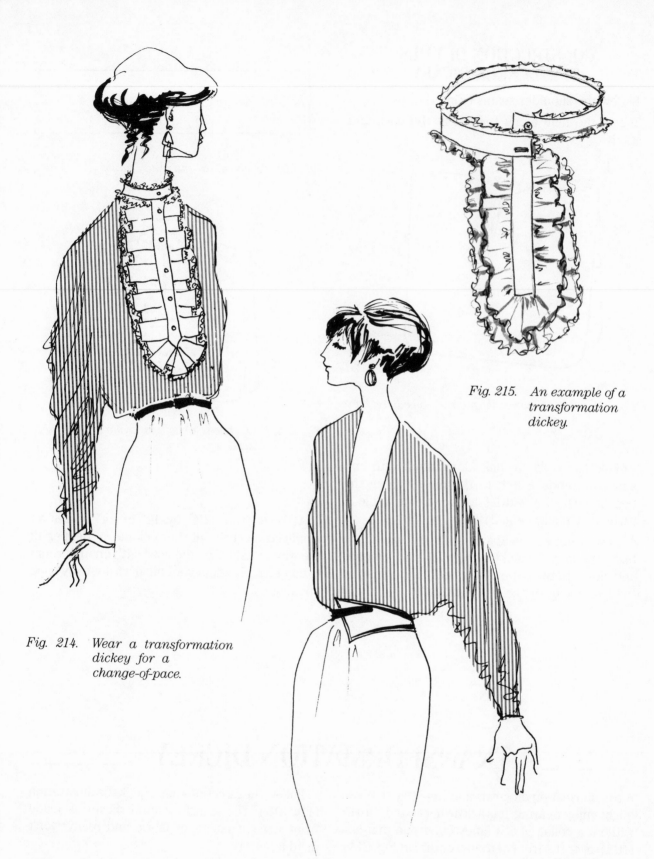

Fig. 214. *Wear a transformation
dickey for a
change-of-pace.*

Fig. 215. *An example of a
transformation
dickey.*

1. For the neckband and facing, cut two strips of fabric, 16″ long by 2″ wide (Fig. 216).

2. This dickey can be made with the plain, banded neckline or a ruffled band at the neck. To add a collar, cut and interface two strips of fabric 14″ long by 3″ wide; interface the collar (Fig. 217).

3. For the front tab, you will need an interfaced strip of fabric, 8″ long by 2½″ wide (Fig. 218). To facilitate buttoning the dickey to the front of a shirt, make evenly spaced, machine buttonholes down the middle of the tab. Check the button spacing on several of your blouses to arrive at a buttonhole spacing that will adjust to different garments.

4. Ruffling for collarbands and front tabs is sewn between the outer part and the facing. The trim can either be preruffled (purchased) eyelet, ruffled lace of any width, or strips of matching fabric that you can ruffle on your sewing machine.

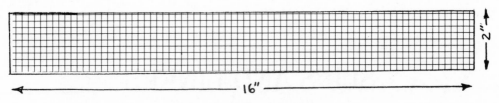

Fig. 216. Cut two strips of fabric for the neckband and facing.

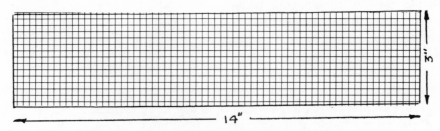

Fig. 217. Dimensions for the dickey collar.

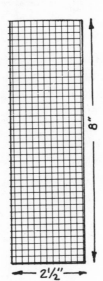

Fig. 218. Add this tab to the collarband.

The outer edges of the body of the dickey can either be overcast with the zigzag stitch from your regular sewing machine or run through the serger.

Add string ties or elastic at each side to connect the front and back for more comfortable wearing.

To make your own double ruffling: Cut a strip of fabric twice the length of the band (16″) by 1½″ wide; cut an additional strip, 34″ long by 3½″ wide. Finish the edges on 3 sides, either with a rolled hem or narrow lace. Run a long basting stitch along the fourth side and draw up the stitching to fit the tab. Sew one narrow and one wide strip to each side of the front tab between the tab and facing. Attach ruffled tab to the front of the neckband. Complete the buttonholes. Sew a button at the neckband to close the collar. Button to the existing buttons of a shirt.

To wear over a sweater or other buttonless garment, insert dress-shirt studs into the empty buttonholes of the dickey. Button the collarband and give a completely new look to something that may have been in your wardrobe for years.

SLIPS AND LINERS

A slip to make your skirt hang nicely can magically result from any skirt pattern or the same two measurements used to create your basic skirt pattern in this book. You can even make a half-slip by cutting a nylon nightgown that you no longer wear. Measure along the seam lines from the bottom of the existing hem to your preferred skirt length (Fig. 219). Mark that length with pins, pencil, chalk, or pen. Mark around the entire waist and cut off the excess fabric at the top of the nightgown. The upper section can be hemmed and used as a camisole. If the top is too short, add a wide strip of edging lace or prehemmed eyelet at the bottom.

To complete the lower section or slip, cut a strip of ½″ or ¾″ elastic, 2″ less than your waistline measurement. Stitch it into a ring; then fold it into four quarters to find the center front, center back, and both sides. Pin these points evenly around the upper edge of the slip. Stretch the elastic to fit the fabric as you stitch it to the waist. There is no need to hem the finished slip; you can use the hem of the original nightgown (Fig. 220).

Fig. 219.   Measure from the hemline to create a slip from a nightgown.

Fig. 220.   A slip and camisole made from a night-gown.

HALF-SLIPS

The two measurements used to create the A-line skirt pattern will yield a half-slip with two panels that can be worn in different ways (Fig. 221). There are several ways to make a half-slip from scratch.

Use half of your hip measurement plus 3″ for the width of each panel. Cut two panels for this slip—a front and a back. Each panel is cut straight down from the waist to the hemline.

Your skirt length minus 1″ is a pretty good rule of thumb for the length of the slip. When you cut the slip, curve the four corners at the bottom edges to prevent them from peeking out from a skirt slit.

Contrary to the usual methods for sewing a garment, the finishing is done first for this slip before the waistband is attached. Here are three methods to complete it:

1. Zigzag around the three sides (sides and bottom) of each panel with your regular sewing machine.

2. With an overlock machine, run each panel through the machine bed, using a narrow-width stitch with a two-thread rolled hem as your final finish.

3. The third method of finishing is to sew narrow lace around the three unfinished sides. The lace can either match or contrast with the chosen fabric. Use a narrow zigzag setting on your regular sewing machine and a short stitch (approximately 12 to 14 stitches to the inch). Lay the lace on top of the fabric and stitch around the three sides of the garment, easing the lace gently around the curves at the bottom corners to ensure its lying flat. Cut away the excess fabric from the back.

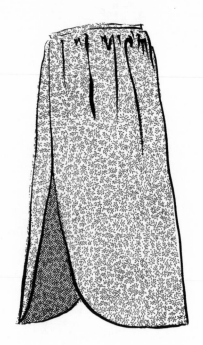

Fig. 221. A two-panel half-slip is very versatile.

142

When you have completed the two panels, you will need elastic for the top of the slip: your waistline measurement minus 2". Overlap the two completed panels by approximately 1" at each side along the unfinished edge and pin them together. Sew the elastic into a ring; then pin elastic to the two sides, the center front, and center back. Stretch the elastic as you sew it to the wrong side of the slip with an elastic stitch or a narrow zigzag. When it is completely attached to the upper edge of the slip, fold the elastic over the stitching to the right side and stitch a second time. This secures the elastic, and backs it, so that it can't pinch your skin on the inside.

Wherever the slits occur in the outer garment, turn in the openings of the slip (Fig. 221). You'll never again experience peekaboo undergarments. This style of slip works well under any style of skirt.

PETTICOATS

Elegant petticoats can be made from lightweight fabrics, using the circle skirt pattern. The radius should be drawn 4" shorter than the actual skirt pattern to allow for a ruffled band around the hem. A 3" ruffle can be sewn at the bottom. Elastic is attached at the waistline. For a square-dance skirt, these petticoats can be worn in multiples of two or more to make the skirt stand out.

To merely underline a full skirt without making it stand away from the body, cut the petticoats from nylon tricot or other soft lingerie fabric and finish the hem with a long zigzag stitch on your sewing machine. You'll have a scalloped hem effect on a simple slip. Lace edging can be substituted for the machine stitching.

The boring world of ecru, black, and white lingerie can now be left behind as new colors are introduced into your wardrobe. Bright colors from your personal color scheme, prints that you'd love to wear but hesitated to add to a rather sedate wardrobe—all this and more can make opening your lingerie drawers an absolute treat. If color influences our every mood, let the influence by happy.

SCARVES

It really isn't necessary to dash out and buy a series of patterns to create scarves. Most of the scarves that accessorize a wardrobe are cut as rectangles or squares. Scarves and belts (more rectangles) of assorted sizes can be dreamed up from leftover pieces of sewing fabrics.

Scarves can be made in a variety of shapes and sizes (Fig. 222). The most commonly found style is the square scarf that can be worn around the head or the neck. Head scarves are best cut in 24" squares to allow enough length at the corners (when folded on the bias) to make a proper tie or knot. Methods for finishing range from a machine-rolled hem to blind-stitching the hem by hand. The quality of fabric used will determine the extent of labor in finishing the scarf.

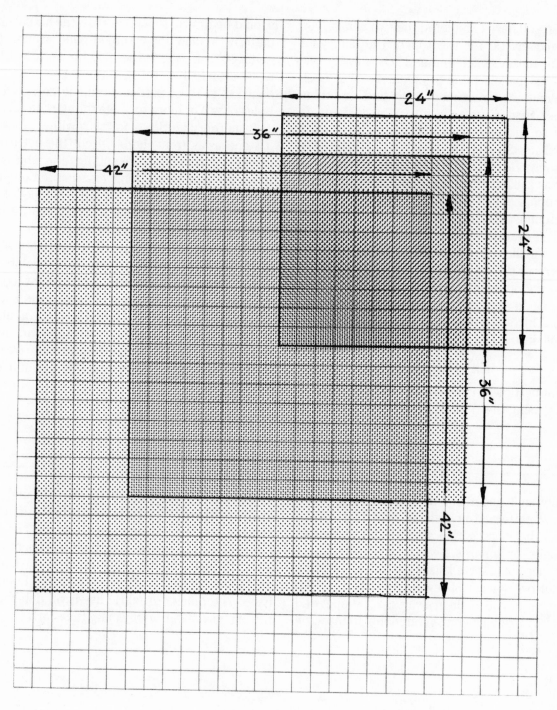

Fig. 222.   Common sizes for square scarves.

Overcast a simple cotton square on a regular sewing machine with a zigzag or decorative stitch; or simply edge-finish your scarf on an overlock machine. Unless you are using some exceptional cotton fabric, it really isn't necessary to use too much time in finishing this type of scarf. You could probably finish a dozen scarves of assorted colors on your sewing machine in less time than it would take to hem one by hand.

Try these cotton squares in a variety of sizes. A 36″ square makes a great summer halter that teams nicely with a dirndl or gathered skirt (Fig. 223) or pants. It can also be draped around your shoulders as a stole on a chilly evening (Fig. 224). It is a comfortable addition to any summer wardrobe and folds like a handkerchief for packing or storage.

Fig. 223. Wear a scarf as a halter.

In a 42″ size, this square can become a pareu or a sarong (Fig. 225). It can easily substitute for a summer dress, skirt, or bathing suit cover-up.

Voluminous triangles of drapey fabric, such as jersey or Qiana nylon will make a lovely wrap for a mild evening. They can be finished with a rolled edge, silky fringe, or various widths of ruffling. Your style of dressing can set the mood for the finishing details of these stoles.

Fig. 224. Drape a large square around your shoulders.

Fig. 225.   Wear a pareu for summer cooling.

A triangle cut from 60″ lace will make two generous shawls—one for your own use and one for a gift. Fold the fabric on the bias and cut along the fold. Raw edges can either be rolled and stitched or encased in matching strips of nylon tricot, a substitute for foldover tape. Edging lace can also be sewn around the three sides, using a short, narrow zigzag stitch. Cut from leftover pieces of crepe or chiffon, these triangles can make a matching evening skirt into a complete outfit (Fig. 226).

A length of wool mohair gives about the same warmth as a short coat when worn over a suit jacket in winter. Carefully measure the width of the fabric and buy that exact amount of length to make a square. Soft mohair weaves, such as angora, vary in width from the usual 36″, 45″, or 54″ due to elasticity of the yarn.

Any of these loosely woven fabrics can be self-fringed very easily. Decide how deep you want your fringe to be and pull threads evenly along each side.

Mohair triangles can also be hemmed by machine or bound with foldover braid or strips of leather. If you can't find leather strips by the yard, cut them yourself from a skin of the appropriate color. Ultrasuede fabric also makes nice edging; and a few extra inches could yield a matching

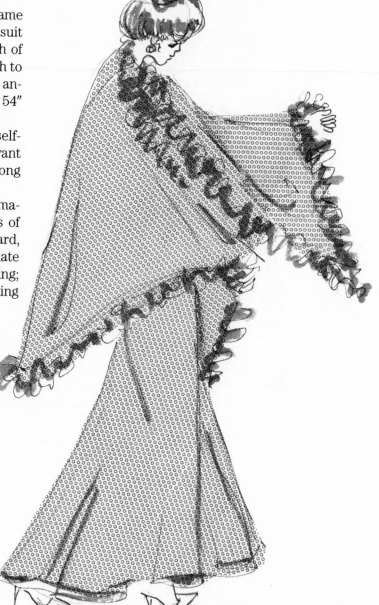

Fig. 226.   Match a stole to your evening skirt.

belt. These strips can also be folded over the raw edges of the fabric, encasing them in a handsome finish.

Long scarves can be used in many ways. Tie one around your waist and you have a colorful belt; under a collar it substitutes for a tie; around your head it becomes a decorative headband, a perfect substitute for a hat. Long scarves can either be cut on the bias or with the grain of the fabric. When making a straight scarf of 45″ to 60″, cut it from the cross grain of the fabric. This saves fabric and can be made from as little as 10″ of actual yardage length (Fig. 227).

A truly luxurious wrap can be made from one yard of 60″ cotton or wool knit. Finish all four sides on your sewing machine and gather the short ends as tightly as possible. Make pompons or tassels from yarn and attach them firmly to the gathered ends (Fig. 228). When you've made this wrap once, you'll probably want it in a variety of colors. Make one from challis. It would be a lovely addition to your wardrobe and go with a multitude of garments.

Fig. 227.   An assortment of long scarves.

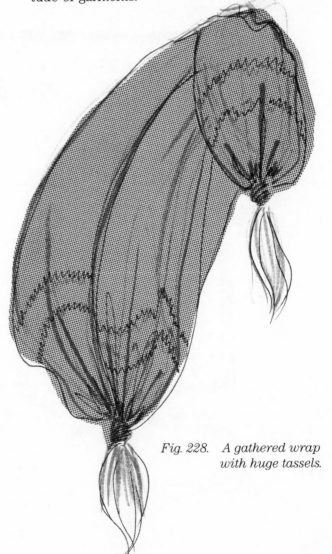

Fig. 228.   A gathered wrap with huge tassels.

BELTS

A belt can be as simple as a piece of fabric or a length of ribbon or rope knotted around the waist. It can also be a handsome and decorative accessory made from leather or Ultrasuede fabric and an unusual buckle (Fig. 229). The important thing to know before starting a belt is your actual waistline measurement. The amount of overlap for the belt will be determined by the style chosen.

Woven belting can form an attractive belt with the addition of two D-rings at one end (Fig. 230). The rings should be of a size to easily accept the belting. Two-inch belting can be slipped through 1″ or 1½″ D-rings by pleating the ends. Fringe the loose end. Allow 4″ to 6″ more than your waist measurement for the length of this style.

Fig. 229. Almost anything can be worn at the waist.

Leather or Ultrasuede fabric can be used in 1″ to 3″ widths to create some very colorful and washable belts. They can be worn just as you cut them (without stitching of any kind). Tie each end in a square knot to wear the belt immediately. The addition of some type of buckle completely changes the mood of these belts (Fig. 231). Wider belts can be lined with fabric or suede of a contrasting color to make the belt reversible. These are usually worn crushed down to a comfortable height.

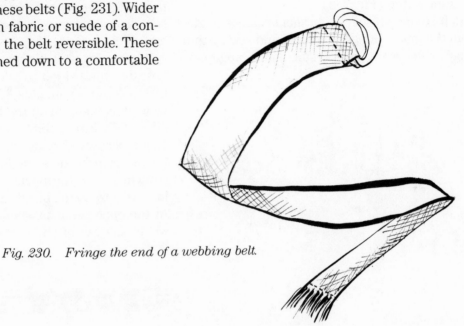

Fig. 230.   Fringe the end of a webbing belt.

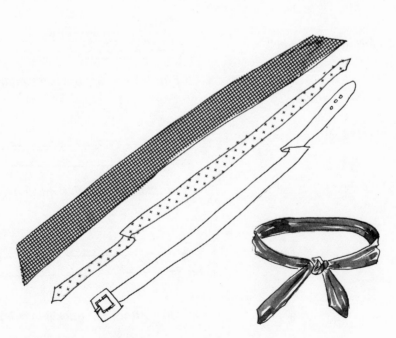

Fig. 231.   An assortment of quick belts.

Elastic belts are put together with an interlocking buckle and a length of decorative elastic belting, long enough to go around the waist. For a belt, use the actual waistline measurement for the elastic length. Fold ¾" to 1" of belting over the bracket and each section of the buckle; then machine-stitch (Fig. 232).

Belts to match specific garments can be made from the fabric along the selvage and sewing the lengthwise seam with right sides together (Fig. 233). Turn the tube to the right side and press firmly with the seam at the middle of the fabric length (Fig. 234). At this point in the construction, you can topstitch around the long sides and one end (Fig. 235). The buckle is attached at the open end of the belt. Slip the fabric through the metal loop of the buckle, fold to the wrong side, and stitch across the fabric with a zipper foot as close to the loop as possible (Fig. 236).

When using a buckle that has a prong, punch a hole into the belting to admit the prong. Punch that hole approximately ¾" to 1" from the raw edge, depending upon the belting you are using (Fig. 237). Firm fabrics and leather need less length because they don't ravel. To fasten, insert the prong in the hole and fold the fabric over the straight bar of the buckle; stitch with a zipper foot, as close to the buckle as possible (Fig. 238). At the opposite or finished end, mark the point where the tail of the belt overlaps the buckle.

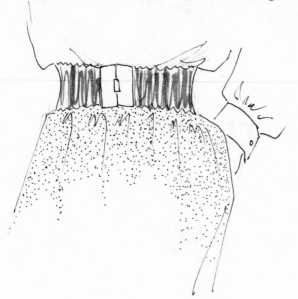

Fig. 232.   Make a comfortable elastic belt.

Fig. 233.   Sew the lengthwise seam.

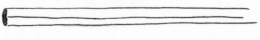

Fig. 234.   Press the belt centering the seam.

Fig. 235.   Topstitch the belt around three sides.

Fig. 236.   Attach the buckle to complete the belt.

Insert an eyelet at this point. Bracket with eyelets on either side of the one you originally inserted to allow for waistline adjustments (Fig. 239).

Accessories are wardrobe picker-uppers and also quick to sew. They are the least expensive items to sew and can often be created from left-over fabrics and trimmings. Accessories are a wonderful place to let one's imagination run rampant. Be wild and lighthearted with your accessories. Test new colors and ideas and put fun back into your wardrobe.

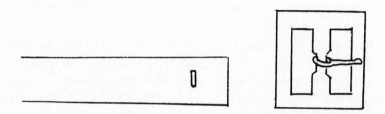

Fig. 237.   Punch a hole to admit the buckle prong.

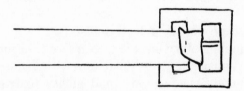

Fig. 238.   Sew the buckle to the belting.

Fig. 239.   Insert eyelets at end of belt.

Epilogue

Fashion is a living thing; it grows and changes as life itself. It can be exciting, pleasurable, and inspiring. New styles and ideas grow from the seeds of what was created yesterday. New trends develop from simple changes—the position of a hemline or the addition of shoulder pads. There are great rewards for whatever effort is expended, not the least of which is the sense of pride that comes from wearing a creation of your own hand.

Personal fashion begins with proper fit, individually suitable color, and complimentary lines; it is personal vision, a created image, an interpretation of a private state of mind. True fashion is moving that germ of an idea, that secret concept of self, from the back of the mind to the finished product that graces your body as you proudly enter a room.

Take the best of seasonal fashion offerings and put it to work for you. Develop a personal signature for your wardrobe. Wear clothes that have the fit and lines that proffer the maximum flattery. Gather the colors and designs that express your personality and compliment your body structure. Wear your choices with flair and confidence.

Nurture your imagination and allow your ideas to flow with a sense of humor. Expand your desire and ability to truly *see* (not just look at) the things that can brighten your day.

METRIC EQUIVALENCY CHART

MM—MILLIMETRES   CM—CENTIMETRES

INCHES TO MILLIMETRES AND CENTIMETRES

INCHES	MM	CM	INCHES	CM	INCHES	CM
⅛	3	0.3	9	22.9	30	76.2
¼	6	0.6	10	25.4	31	78.7
⅜	10	1.0	11	27.9	32	81.3
½	13	1.3	12	30.5	33	83.8
⅝	16	1.6	13	33.0	34	86.4
¾	19	1.9	14	35.6	35	88.9
⅞	22	2.2	15	38.1	36	91.4
1	25	2.5	16	40.6	37	94.0
1¼	32	3.2	17	43.2	38	96.5
1½	38	3.8	18	45.7	39	99.1
1¾	44	4.4	19	48.3	40	101.6
2	51	5.1	20	50.8	41	104.1
2½	64	6.4	21	53.3	42	106.7
3	76	7.6	22	55.9	43	109.2
3½	89	8.9	23	58.4	44	111.8
4	102	10.2	24	61.0	45	114.3
4½	114	11.4	25	63.5	46	116.8
5	127	12.7	26	66.0	47	119.4
6	152	15.2	27	68.6	48	121.9
7	178	17.8	28	71.1	49	124.5
8	203	20.3	29	73.7	50	127.0

YARDS TO METRES

YARDS	METRES	YARDS	METRES	YARDS	METRES	YARDS	METRES	YARDS	METRES
⅛	0.11	2⅛	1.94	4⅛	3.77	6⅛	5.60	8⅛	7.43
¼	0.23	2¼	2.06	4¼	3.89	6¼	5.72	8¼	7.54
⅜	0.34	2⅜	2.17	4⅜	4.00	6⅜	5.83	8⅜	7.66
½	0.46	2½	2.29	4½	4.11	6½	5.94	8½	7.77
⅝	0.57	2⅝	2.40	4⅝	4.23	6⅝	6.06	8⅝	7.89
¾	0.69	2¾	2.51	4¾	4.34	6¾	6.17	8¾	8.00
⅞	0.80	2⅞	2.63	4⅞	4.46	6⅞	6.29	8⅞	8.12
1	0.91	3	2.74	5	4.57	7	6.40	9	8.23
1⅛	1.03	3⅛	2.86	5⅛	4.69	7⅛	6.52	9⅛	8.34
1¼	1.14	3¼	2.97	5¼	4.80	7¼	6.63	9¼	8.46
1⅜	1.26	3⅜	3.09	5⅜	4.91	7⅜	6.74	9⅜	8.57
1½	1.37	3½	3.20	5½	5.03	7½	6.86	9½	8.69
1⅝	1.49	3⅝	3.31	5⅝	5.14	7⅝	6.97	9⅝	8.80
1¾	1.60	3¾	3.43	5¾	5.26	7¾	7.09	9¾	8.92
1⅞	1.71	3⅞	3.54	5⅞	5.37	7⅞	7.20	9⅞	9.03
2	1.83	4	3.66	6	5.49	8	7.32	10	9.14

Index